The Save Your Business Book

The Save Your Business Book

A *Survival Manual for Small Business Owners*

John Goldhammer

LEXINGTON BOOKS
An Imprint of Macmillan, Inc.
New York

Maxwell Macmillan Canada
Toronto

Maxwell Macmillan International
New York   Oxford   Singapore   Sydney

Library of Congress Cataloging-in-Publication Data

Goldhammer, John D.
　　The save your business book : a survival manual for small business owners
/ by John D. Goldhammer.
　　　　p.　cm.
　　Includes bibliographical references.
　　ISBN 0-02-912-115-9
　　1. Corporate turnarounds—Management.　　2. Small business—Management.
I. Title
HD58.8.G62　　1993
658.4'063—dc20　　　　　　　　　　　　　　　　　　　　92–32074
　　　　　　　　　　　　　　　　　　　　　　　　　　　　CIP

Lexington Books
An Imprint of Macmillan, Inc.
866 Third Avenue, New York, N.Y. 10022

Maxwell Macmillan Canada, Inc.
1200 Eglinton Avenue East
Suite 200
Don Mills, Ontario M3C 3N1

Macmillan, Inc. is part of the Maxwell Communication Group of Companies.

Printed in the United States of America
1　2　3　4　5　6　7　8　9　10

To my father
who taught me there is no such word as "can't"

Contents

PART ONE

Avoiding Bankruptcy

PART TWO

Reorganizing Your Business

PART THREE

Declaring Bankruptcy

List of Exhibits

Author Note

I have made every effort to provide you with useful, accurate and timely information in this handbook. However, the law in this area is based upon a combination of federal and state statutes that are highly complex as well as subject to frequent changes and variations from state to state. Consequently, a book such as this must, by its nature, often deal in generalities. It cannot guarantee total applicability to all sets of circumstances nor be expected to serve as a substitute for the services of an attorney or other professional when they are required. Readers should be guided accordingly. For more detailed information, please refer to the sources listed in Appendix A of this book.

Introduction

According to Dun & Bradstreet, 7,272 American firms failed each month of 1991, a 44% increase over 1990, setting a record exceeded only by the Great Depression.[1]

The need for a practical hands-on business survival guide is overwhelming. Business failures in the United States are increasing at an alarming rate. Bankruptcies of the largest corporations are now commonplace events. Many thousands of business firms operate on the brink of financial disaster, eventually closing their doors or, in many cases, being absorbed by larger companies. Numerous giant corporations have been forced to file bankruptcy: Penn Central, W. T. Grant & Company, the Manville Corporation, Braniff Airlines, and more recently Drexel Burnham Lambert, Eastern Air Lines, Pan Am, Texaco, and LTV Corporation, to name just a few.

In 1991, 87,266 U.S. business firms failed, compared to 10,622 in 1981. The liabilities of bankrupt companies drastically increased to $108.8 billion in 1991, compared to $55.5 billion in 1990.[2] Dun & Bradstreet reported that business failures were up 25 percent over 1991 for the first two months of 1992. In the next ten years, it is estimated that over one million business firms will fail. Domestic corporate debt increased from $829 billion in 1980 to over $2 trillion by 1990.[3] In 1991, in Los Angeles alone, business and personal bankruptcies were being filed at the record rate of over 6,500 a month—one filing for every minute of the first four months of 1991.[4]

Bankruptcies are big business for the legal profession. Lawyers are spending an estimated $28 million per year just to advertise bankruptcy services. This advertising blitz is prompting numerous individuals and business firms to file bankruptcy, when it is frequently not the best choice. Many individuals are misled as to the consequences of filing bankruptcy and the stigma resulting from such a public failure.

Luther Gatling, the director of Budget and Credit Counseling of New York, describes the typical modern-day debtor:

> Now we see a new kind of debtor. He's an overextended survivor, rather than an overextended debtor. He has a good credit rating, prides himself on paying his bills. And his life style has not altered. It's increased living costs that got him. None of these people are deadbeats, and most never had a credit problem five years ago. We get Ph.D.'s, architects, all walks of life, all races. You'd be amazed how many investment counselors we see. Most had no credit problems before. Now they look at each other and ask, " What's happened, why can't we pay our bills?"
> —N.Y. Daily News
>   Aug 26, 1979, P. 5

This book is based on forty years of personal experience with both failure and success in the business world. As a young boy, I had an intense interest in becoming an entrepreneur and was always starting small business enterprises—from growing mushrooms to making rubber stamps "for fun and profit," just as the advertisement promised. Needless to say, my early business ventures taught me a lot but did not make me wealthy. By the time I graduated from high school, I had accumulated some pretty interesting job experiences. A paper route lasted a short time; when winter arrived, getting up at 3 A.M. and pushing a bicycle loaded down with papers through two feet of snow convinced me to look for different work. I spent a couple of summers mixing huge vats of concentrated syrup for a vending-machine company. One summer I had a job cleaning telephone booths—the old-fashioned glass and aluminum type with folding doors; I earned seventy-five cents per booth. Another summer I worked selling tickets at a neighborhood drive-in theater. My last year in high school, I worked as an apprentice draftsman for a construction company.

After a brief stint in college, my formal business experience began with management training for the F. W. Woolworth Co., where I quickly worked my way from the stockroom to the management level. Later, my brother and I purchased a small office-supply business with one employee and total sales of $95,000 per year. We literally worked day and night, going to work before sunrise and returning home in the dark. As the business grew, I worked in every area of the operation, from taking orders, wrapping packages, and unloading trucks, to planning and opening branch stores, developing a successful mail-order division, and installing computerized accounting systems. But hard work payed off, and within a few years, sales reached the multimillion-dollar level with substantial profits and benefits.

After selling my share of this business in 1978, I started an office furniture and design business that did well until the 1982 recession. In 1984, after a panic-filled two-year struggle, my business failed. I lost everything in the process, including most of my self-esteem. Deciding to change professions and also make use of my business experience, I found part-time accounting work and returned to college full time, obtaining two degrees, one in accounting and the other in management information systems.

While in the process of going back to school, I began to realize the many ways I could have survived my business failure. I also realized what a valuable experience it had been; I had learned priceless lessons from two opposite sets of circumstances; failure and success. At this point I determined to write of my experiences, knowing that had I had access to a book of this sort, it would have changed everything: I knew that I could have saved and revitalized my business if I had simply had the right information at the right time. So I began writing and researching the material for *The Save Your Business Book.*

Through direct experience in my own business ventures, I learned the methods explained in the following chapters, usually after much trial and error—usually too late to do any good. It is my hope to save you from making many of the same mistakes I made and, in the process, save *your* business.

Business problems can become very trying, but positive changes are often the result of chaotic, difficult circumstances in life. It is important not to let a potential business failure get blown out of proportion. A failure in business is not the end of the world. In fact, it can be a new birth, a new beginning. The possibility of a failure looming over one's head can be the catalyst in life that gets one out of complacency and dead-end attitudes and situations. There is a story:

There once lived a very rich and powerful king who, in spite of his vast riches, still experienced the ups and downs of life without very much peace of mind. He determined to find a solution to these inevitable swings of joy and despair, love and hatred.

One day he ordered his palace jeweler to consult with his astrologer and adviser and to design a ring that would give him this much-sought-after equanimity and peace of mind. Several months passed, and the king became ever more curious and impatient to see what they had designed. The day finally arrived and they presented the king with a simple gold ring. The jeweler explained to the king that whenever he experienced either grief or joy, to read the inscription on his ring. On the ring were these words: "This too shall pass."[5]

No business difficulty is permanent; it will pass. However, we can prolong our difficulties for a long time through doing nothing. In the business world, delay in facing any problem is a guarantee that things are going to get worse.

Nothing is worse than the sinking feeling that comes with money troubles. It is a feeling of helplessness and real frustration! It is good to remember that success or failure in the business world is not a measure of individual character or integrity. It is our modern society that so often gauges a person's accomplishments based on monetary accumulation. We can easily fall victim to this faulty view of life and consider ourselves failures when we fail to measure up to society's standards. If money were the true basis of gauging an individual's worth, then any drug dealer or criminal could belong to the accepted and honored ranks of "successful" persons. The true and only lasting success is how we *live* life—with integrity, honesty, and helping in some way to make this earth a better home for our children.

It is in *trying*—making the best effort possible to work our way out of the financial problems we face—that we really succeed or fail. The only real failure is giving up—not trying. Saving your business is secondary to saving your self-esteem, and whether your business ultimately succeeds or fails, it is most important that *you survive* with the right sense of values about the business of life. If this is the result, you will be a success in the sight of the person who counts most: yourself. Albert Einstein once wrote regarding success, "Try not to become a man of success but rather try to become a man of value."

So don't panic and don't let anyone push you into making any choices that are not carefully and rationally worked out. Many persons, under extreme pressure from banks and creditors, rush prematurely into bankruptcy proceedings. The fear caused by not knowing how the law works and what attorneys can do through suits and other legal steps can push a business or an individual into bankruptcy when it is not necessary. There are many things you can do right now to help save your business, your own sense of self-worth, and your integrity.

We have only to glance at history to see that those individuals whose work has brought some lasting good are those whose lives have inspired others and encouraged people to live with ethics, compassion, and understanding. If your business is in trouble, you're in good company. Some very prominent businesses as well as individuals have failed financially. Carl Sandburg, writing in his biography of Abraham Lincoln, described how "Lincoln at twenty-four years of age had on his hands the airy wrecks and the cold, real debts of three bankrupt stores." Lincoln was eventually able to repay each debt.

The Save Your Business Book is a fact-filled, hands-on business survival guide that tells you exactly how to get out of financial difficulty fast, how to profitably reorganize your business affairs, how to protect your business assets from legal assaults, how to increase profits, and how to manage your business more effectively. It explains the alternatives to bankruptcy and the advantages and dangers of each alternative. It shows you exactly how to stop financial pressure from creditors immediately and to transform a negative cash flow into a positive one. There are ways to increase your cash flow and operating capital without borrowing a cent. There are ways to hold off creditors without filing bankruptcy so that you have valuable time to resolve your business problems in an orderly manner.

In the following chapters, we will examine the most critical steps of operating a business: cash management, planning, budgeting and forecasting, internal controls, personnel, selling, pricing, marketing, and advertising. In addition, we will explore ways to deal with the emotional and psychological impact that business troubles always produce. We will take a look at "failure," "success," and changing values as we approach the twenty-first century. We will look at ways to cope with panic, fear, and stress—how to keep your cool when everything around you is falling apart. I explain what to watch out for in troubled times so that you do not become an easy prey to the many unethical individuals in the "scavenger" business who are always on the lookout for a business in trouble.

I will present, step by step, the way to handle a serious business crisis right now. In most situations you will not need the services of an attorney, as the methods explained involve your own reorganization of your financial affairs and not bankruptcy proceedings. However, many varied and unusual circumstances can arise in a time of business difficulty, and you should not hesitate to obtain competent legal advice if you decide it is necessary.

Send In Your Suggestions

I am vitally interested in your feedback, the suggestions and thoughts you may have regarding the procedures set forth in this book. Let me know about your experiences and also any suggestions you have for additions to this book.

PART ONE

Avoiding Bankruptcy

No one knows what he can do till he tries
—Publilius Syrus

1

Alternatives to Bankruptcy

"How did you go bankrupt?" Bill asked.
"Two ways," Mike said. "Gradually and then suddenly."
—*Ernest Hemingway, The Sun Also Rises*

Reasons to Avoid Bankruptcy

There are many important advantages to a nonbankruptcy approach to resolving your financial problems. There is a definite stigma associated with bankruptcy proceedings. Bankruptcy is viewed as a failure by the public and by other business owners. It is seen as a final admission of the inability to work out or solve one's business troubles. Some persons will consider you a cheat and a thief.

A bankruptcy or Chapter 11 reorganization will have negative effects on your customers and your suppliers. Customers like to think that a business will be around in the future to take care of problems and to provide continued products and services. As soon as your customers begin to hear rumors of any financial difficulties, you are very likely to lose business.

It is a fact that you can count on getting far less for your business assets when those assets are auctioned off in a bankruptcy sale than you could get in many nonbankruptcy alternatives. For instance, if you handle the sale of your business equipment, inventory, and other assets, you are likely to get much better prices. In bankruptcy, assets are sold primarily to pay the fees of trustees, attorneys, accountants, and so on. Distress sales such as bankruptcy auctions commonly get 30 to 70 percent of wholesale cost (10 to 30 percent of the retail price), depending on the quality and desirability of the goods.[1] Higher administrative costs, inefficiency, and red tape are the significant drawbacks to most bankruptcy proceedings.

Creditors often prefer that a debtor avoid bankruptcy for the same reasons that a debtor wants to avoid bankruptcy, especially when a business has been a good customer to its suppliers and there is a temporary cash shortage that can be worked out over time. Creditors in this situation are usually more than willing to make considerable concessions to help a business get back on its feet financially.

An important psychological aspect is involved as well: your own self-esteem. You will be better off in the future if you do everything in your power to save your business. Whether you succeed or fail, you will be at peace with yourself.

There is a strong possibility that a business bankruptcy will trigger a personal bankruptcy as well, poisoning your credit record for the next ten years. You can lose your home and most assets and still end up having to pay taxes, alimony, child support, and certain other obligations that are not exempt under bankruptcy laws.

Making the Right Decision

Bankruptcy is not the only answer to a financial crisis. It is frequently possible to straighten out a severe business or personal money crisis through other methods. You must ask yourself what you really want to do, keeping in mind the consequences of your decision. Entering bankruptcy proceedings is a step not to be taken lightly. It has far-reaching consequences that will affect your life for many years to come.

In making a decision, one of the simplest and best ways is to make two columns on a sheet of paper. List the advantages on one side and the disadvantages on the other side. Be thorough and write down every detail and all potential outcomes. Then give yourself some time to sleep on it—to really digest the alternatives and consequences—before you decide on a course of action.

We will now look at the alternatives to bankruptcy. Ultimately you must make a choice, and I intend to do everything possible to enable you to make the right one for your particular situation. You can make the right choice only after carefully considering all the options available and receiving a good understanding of the consequences that will result from each choice. The only wrong choice is the choice based on ignorance, pressure, panic, or fear. Every choice has its consequences. Regardless of your decision, there is a price tag attached—a price tag for continuing the status quo, and a price tag for changing your situation for the better.

Questions to Ask

You should ask yourself these questions to help find the potential difficulties that lie ahead and your strong points. However, with a total commitment you should view any obstacle not as insurmountable, but as a challenge to your creativity and ingenuity:

1. Will my suppliers continue to provide the critical services and products needed for the continued operation of my business, while accepting extended terms of payment? Do I have other sources of supply that are easily available?

This is a potential problem area and will depend to a large extent upon how your suppliers see you as an ethical and responsible individual. This sort of evaluation will be based on their past and present business dealings with your company. Have you been direct and honest and paid bills on time for the most part, and have you kept your word in all situations? The cooperation of your most important suppliers is a significant help in the reorganization of your business affairs.

2. Do I have any large creditors who might begin legal action when I attempt to reorganize my affairs?

There is always the potential for a large creditor or group of creditors to initiate bankruptcy proceedings, especially if there is a substantial risk involved, or if they do not trust your ability to turn around your business. This danger can be quickly defused with the proper approach to your creditors.

In Chapter 2, I explain in detail exactly how to approach your suppliers so that they will trust your efforts and understand that they have more to lose via the bankruptcy approach than through your reorganization plan. In fact, most suppliers dread bankruptcy proceedings and are more than willing to work with you in the reorganization of your affairs. It is the lack of any plan and apparent inaction on your part that often frightens large suppliers into taking some type of legal action. Once you offer a solution to them, you will find the vast majority are relieved.

3. Are the general business conditions favorable for reorganization? In other words, is the local competition making it impossible for me to sell my product or services at a reasonable profit? Is my business in a dying industry?

If so, your only real choice may be to liquidate and get into another line of work.

4. Do my financial problems have their origin from within my business or from outside market forces?

You have limited means to change the outer business climate in your particular field, but you have many ways to transform problems whose origin is within your own company. In short, a poor outer business environment means a much more difficult reorganization, whereas problems primarily within your business are just opportunities in disguise waiting for a creative solution.

5. Do others see me as a responsible business person with sound business common sense?

If they do, you will enjoy valuable support and help in your efforts. The basic trust of your integrity, honesty, and sound judgment is a valuable asset and gives you a significant boost in starting your reorganization. Lacking this trust from your suppliers, you could have a difficult but not impossible job ahead in negotiations with suppliers.

6. Are my employees competent, and specifically, do they possess the skills necessary to contribute in a constructive way to a reorganization? Are they emotionally and mentally up to the task? Do I have their trust so that they will stay with me when things look darkest?

7. Am I up to the job of rehabilitation?

You must consider your own emotional stamina. Can you call on the inner warrior in your nature to see a reorganization through to completion? Are you both patient and persevering? Are you easily discouraged? How well do you hold up under stress and pressure? Are you a good negotiator?

Your situation may require you to hire temporary or permanent help in certain departments. I am not suggesting hiring a turnaround specialist or "hatchet," but you may need a better bookkeeper, warehouse manager, or accountant. Your shipping department or any other division may need more competent help. A vital part of your reorganization efforts should be an evaluation of your present staff. Are they the best possible people to help you survive?

You can work with your creditors, reorganizing your business affairs in a manner designed to pay your debts gradually. This approach is the most desirable because you save your business and honorably pay your debts. Even if it is ultimately necessary to file bankruptcy, your conscience will be clear for having done your best to save your company.

Bankruptcy Alternatives

Self-Liquidation

In a self-liquidation, you simply sell all business assets, pay all your bills, and close shop. Obviously, you should not consider this method unless your combined assets are sufficient to pay all outstanding debts and trade creditors, especially those to whom you are personally liable. It can be a speedy solution—an easy way out—but only provided you have the necessary resources. If you are depending on the money raised from a liquidation sale to pay your bills, you must be absolutely sure that you know in advance what the proceeds will be.

ADVANTAGES. The advantages of a self-liquidation are that it's simple and you avoid the expense, stigma, often lengthy legal proceedings that go with filing bankruptcy. People do not think of a self-liquidation as a bankruptcy. They see a business that has a liquidation sale and simply closes its doors. Perhaps the owners have moved or opened a new business elsewhere. When you control the sale of your business assets, you are likely to get higher prices for the sale than you would in a bankruptcy auction that is handled by a court-appointed trustee. A self-liquidation enables you to move on with most of your reputation and dignity still intact.

DISADVANTAGES. The major disadvantage of a self-liquidation is that you are out of business and out of work, and so are your employees. Depending on the size of your business, this can send shock waves through a community or neighborhood. You may not be very popular if twenty of your neighbors lose their jobs as a result of your decision. You might possibly have saved your business by looking at other alternatives and with more effort and patience.

Your lease is a potential stumbling block and could end up being a substantial financial drain if you are unable to terminate it either through subletting the space or changing the lease agreement. What happens if you break your lease? You may have to find another tenant before actually shutting down operations. In some situations, a landlord can easily rent a particular property at a higher rate than is being paid by the present occupant, especially if the lease or rental rate has remained unchanged for a long period of time. In any event, before proceeding with a self-liquidation, you will need to thoroughly check out your lease agreement.

The choice of self-liquidation may expose even an incorporated business to extensive and protracted legal entanglements, unless you pay a substantial percentage of all bills, loans, and debts. In a self-liquidation, you do not have the legal protection from your creditors that a formal bankruptcy filing gives you.

TAX CONSEQUENCES. The tax consequences of a liquidation revolve around gains or losses on the assets that are sold. The IRS does allow you to deduct losses, but the gain or loss must be figured separately for each asset or type of asset. For example, the gain or loss from selling a restaurant's depreciated kitchen equipment requires a different tax treatment from selling out a store's retail inventory, which results in ordinary income or loss. You may have actual taxable gains even at rock-bottom sale prices on certain depreciable assets if most or all of the depreciation has been taken and the resulting book value or "adjusted basis" is below the sale price. How these losses are treated is further complicated by the structure of the liquidating business: corporation, partnership, or sole proprietorship. You should enlist the help of your accountant or a professional tax adviser before beginning any liquidation. Also be sure any pension plans are fully funded. If pensions are not fully funded, the company owner is liable.

PROCEDURE. Briefly, you need to follow these basic steps in planning and implementing a self-liquidation of your business:

1. Find out *exactly* how much money a liquidation sale will produce. You will need to take a complete and accurate inventory of all assets and have these assets accurately appraised. A liquidator may be hired to give a guaranteed price which may be more reliable than an auction.

2. Assuming you will have sufficient funds to repay all creditors in full, you should consult with your accountant or tax professional regarding the tax consequences of a liquidation.

3. Check your local state agencies to see if any licenses or permits are required to conduct a going-out-of-business sale. Many states now require some type of permit that will protect consumers from business firms that have "going-out-of-business" sales more than once.

4. Check contracts you have signed: loans, leases, equipment rentals or leases, and employment or union contracts. You may liquidate your business but find yourself still paying for the leased phone system. Every lease or contract has to be terminated and the equipment returned or settled in some way before you conduct a liquidation sale. If you have a bank loan, what is the collateral? You may not be able to liquidate inventory or equipment that is collateral for a loan without paying off the loan first. Of course, you cannot sell any leased or consignment inventory because these items do not legally belong to you. Check carefully whether there are security deposits you could recover, or personal guarantees that may follow you—making you personally liable.

5. Having successfully worked through all of the above, you are ready to plan the actual liquidation event, arrange advertising if necessary, and to decide when and where to liquidate all of your assets and how many days or weeks it will realistically take. For instance, in retailing, weekends are often the days with the highest traffic count. Depending on where you are located, there may be a better location to have a sale. The better your planning, the smoother everything will operate. Consider a bulk sale to a liquidator who will take all your inventory or equipment so that you will not be left with unsaleable "junk" at the end.

Assignments—for the Benefit of Whom?

In some states, an *assignment for the benefit of creditors* is an alternative to bankruptcy. Here again, you must check your local state laws. This method is not in use very much today. An assignment for the benefit of creditors is a variation of a self-liquidation. The major difference is that you voluntarily transfer your assets to an assignee. The assignee then sells the assets and distributes the proceeds to your creditors. The consent of your creditors is not required for an assignment of your assets. However, most states require that any assignments be nonpreferential. This means that a valid assignment must be for the benefit of *all* creditors and not show any preferential treatment of one creditor or any group of creditors. In some situations property that is transferred preferentially to a creditor just before an assignment can be recovered from the creditor.

In an assignment for the benefit of creditors, you give up any claim to or control over the property transferred to the assignee. In this type of action, all business assets are immediately sold and the operations of the business come to an abrupt halt except for the completion of certain work in progress. It is rare that an assignee will agree to oversee the continued operations of a business beyond the very short time period necessary to fulfill existing sales contracts or orders. A public auction or sale is the most common method employed in liquidating the assets.

ADVANTAGES. Once the property is legally transferred to the assignee, it cannot be attached by your creditors. However, the law becomes complex in dealing with the types of property transferred and what type of property is still subject to attachment by a creditor, and *you should not consider an assignment without competent legal advice.* This method avoids bankruptcy and still protects you from most creditors.

DISADVANTAGES. An important disadvantage of this type of liquidation is that if a creditor receives from the assignee less than the amount owed, the debt is still not discharged, and your business is not released from liability. An assignment does not by itself protect you against litigations. To prevent this situation, assignment agreements must be drawn up to stipulate that the debtor *is* released from any further liability—but getting creditors to agree to this release is often difficult. Creditors who do not agree to participate in the assignment agreement create complex legal problems for the business owner. Legal skirmishes can drag out the final resolution of a liquidation, causing a lot of grief and potential further financial losses for the owner. Again, laws vary in different areas concerning the type of property that may still be subject to attachment by creditors. Thus it is necessary to get good legal help with assignments.

Assignments for the benefit of creditors do not usually apply to property in which there is a security interest, such as a piece of equipment that is security for an equipment loan. Therefore, this type of liquidation leaves many potential loopholes that can make a final liquidation very difficult unless there are sufficient assets to pay all claims, both secured and unsecured.

A big disadvantage of an assignment is that it may cause creditors to file an involuntary bankruptcy proceeding against you. An involuntary proceeding means that your creditors, not you, have initiated the action. This action is usually initiated by dissenting creditors, who are not paid in full, and commonly happens after the assignment is complete and the assets are sold. The assignee will usually hold all cash raised from the sale of assets for at least 90 days in anticipation of potential involuntary bankruptcy proceedings filed by those creditors who did not agree to the assignment in the first place.

Except in unusual circumstances, an auction will usually bring much less than a going-out-of-business sale. People at business liquidation auctions expect to purchase items at practically giveaway prices. With a going-out-of-business sale, you still have a semblance of a normal sale that will usually attract average shoppers who are willing to pay more. With a business sale, you also have more time to sell at prices set and controlled by you as opposed to the prices at an auction, where everything goes immediately to the highest bidder. An auction is an advantage only if you have unusual assets that might be collectors' items.

TAX CONSEQUENCES. One interesting tax disadvantage is the taxable income created for the business owner when a debt is reduced or a partial payment is accepted as full payment of an obligation. The theory is that what you don't have to pay out is income to you. There are exceptions to this rule, one being when a debt is canceled in the form of a voluntary gift; then the law does not consider it income. Again, this method is complex and you would need good legal and tax help before even considering it.

Composition Agreements

A composition agreement is a legal proceeding where you contract with your creditors to resolve your debts at an agreed-upon lower price, usually with extended time payments. The agreed-upon lower price is the same percentage for all unsecured creditors in the agreement. The amount of the reduction in debt and improvement of cash flow must be enough to result in the rehabilitation of your company. Because of the unique circumstances making up the financial structure of a particular company, the amount of the discount among debtor companies may vary widely and is a subject of major consideration for the creditors. The bigger the discount, the more difficult it will be to get all creditors to agree. Discounts range from as little as 10 percent to 50 percent or more in extreme cases. This approach is best when the total number of creditors is not too great. Composition agreements are really simple contracts and are enforceable as such under the law.

A composition agreement usually begins when your attorney contacts your major creditors and arranges a meeting where the details of an agreement can be worked out. This type of agreement must involve at least two creditors to be valid. You should obtain the help of a lawyer, at least to help you in filling out the necessary paperwork.

A variation of the composition agreement is sometimes called a *creditor's agreement* or a *workout agreement*. The primary difference is the lack of a reduced amount accepted in payment for a debt. This type of agreement usually calls for the complete payment of an obligation over an extended time (extension agreement). You simply contract with your creditors to make installment payments on your bills. This has the immediate effect of improving cash flow.

ADVANTAGES. The advantage of this approach is the avoidance of bankruptcy proceedings and the discharge of those creditors who take part in the composition—and, most important, you stay in business. This may be a workable solution for you, particularly if you have only two or three large creditors. A successful agreement can prevent involuntary bankruptcy proceedings. A composition is not a business liquidation. In a composition agreement, you keep possession of your property unless the agreement calls for other arrangements.

Payments can be made from any assets or property. Composition agreements are ordinarily considered binding by the courts on those creditors who participate in the agreements. This is true even though the creditors receive less than they were originally owed. Most states now have a statute similar to Section 1541 of the California Civil Code, which states: "An obligation is extinguished by a release therefrom given to the debtor by the creditor upon a new consideration, or in writing, with or without new consideration." This type of statute means that the court will enforce a composition agreement and prevent a creditor from trying to collect any sum in excess of the amount stipulated in the agreement. Obviously, you need to know the law in your particular state before considering this type of remedy.

DISADVANTAGES. One disadvantage of a composition agreement is the fact that you will have an agreement that does not fully pay each creditor. As a result, future transactions may be difficult because of your loss of credibility with your suppliers. A composition will also not give you the time you need to reorganize your affairs in a carefully planned manner.

Another disadvantage of a composition agreement is that it is not mandatory for all creditors to accept the terms of the agreement. This fact, however, should not prevent you from going ahead with a composition agreement, provided you have the agreement of at least two creditors. As a result, you may still find yourself with considerable problems caused by the remaining creditors who did not take part in the agreement. In addition, a composition agreement may be expensive. You will need the services of a good attorney as well as of an accountant to deal with creditors or a creditors' committee. Creditors usually like composition contracts because they receive immediate payments at minimal legal expense.

TAX CONSEQUENCES. There may be tax complications because of income produced by reduced debts. If depreciated assets are sold in the process of raising extra funds for the payment to creditors, you may have taxable gains or losses. Thus it is necessary to obtain good tax advice before beginning on this type of remedy.

Turnaround Specialists

Another alternative to a normal bankruptcy is a turnaround specialist, or turnaround manager. Turnaround specialists are often called in as a last desperate attempt to revamp a company, and they usually take over as the authority in all matters related to money flowing in or out of a business. This often means immediately firing some employees, restructuring other jobs, shutting down all bill paying except absolute necessities such as federal and state taxes, and initiating very harsh collection methods with customers who owe money to the firm. This specialist then negotiates with major suppliers to get extended payment terms on existing bills.

ADVANTAGES. The primary advantage of hiring a turnaround specialist is the quick-fix potential if you have exhausted other alternatives or know that you lack the necessary business management expertise to effectively reorganize your business. An experienced turnaround specialist can be a vital help, especially one who has actual business-management work experience. Competent new management may improve your business credibility with creditors, but be sure to check experience and credentials carefully before hiring any outside management help. Many turnaround specialists belong to the Turnaround Management Association (see Appendix A) and subscribe to a code of ethics established to prevent abuse by the profession.

Fees vary widely, and many turnaround specialists work with a business owner in setting fees. You should negotiate a fee arrangement that you can afford within the context of your reorganization plans. Be careful how much authority you give to a turnaround specialist. You may decide to keep such an individual in an advisory position only. An Arabic proverb says, "If the camel once gets his nose in the tent, his body will follow."

DISADVANTAGES. A major drawback is that you may not have much of a company left when a turnaround specialist is finished, and you may end up not owning your business or in control of your affairs. Although fees vary, turnaround specialists do not come cheap. Fees as high as $6,000 per day are not uncommon.

Hiring a turnaround specialist means that you usually lose some or all control of the operation of your business. The fact that an outsider takes over the major decision-making function in your business may be demoralizing for your workers, unless it is convincingly presented to employees and creditors as a necessary positive step. In a crisis time the loyalty and support of your employees is a critical factor in the success of any reorganization efforts. The impact of a turnaround specialist on the people in your organization is an important consideration in your choice of this alternative—all the more reason to carefully check the qualifications and references of any individual brought into your business in a managerial position.

You are better off planning your own reorganization, enlisting the support and cooperation of your employees, and proceeding with carefully thought-out compassionate steps that will consider the long-term interests of your business success and the welfare of those who have been loyal workers.

Debt Restructuring

Although primarily used by large companies, debt restructuring is an alternative to bankruptcy—or at least a way to temporarily postpone trouble. Debt restructuring usually involves teams of accountants, lawyers, and bankers who offer a quick fix by rearranging the debt structure of a company, that is, changing the relationship of assets to liabilities on a company's balance sheet. Substantial debt restructuring is, in a way, a partial (informal) bankruptcy reorganization; a company is essentially getting bondholders, investors, or creditors to give up something, usually in exchange for equity ownership. In fact, many debt-restructuring packages are put together to ward off impending involuntary bankruptcy proceedings. Creditors often try the restructuring plan as an alternative to the risk of losing even more or all of their money in an actual bankruptcy. The creditors also postpone taking substantial writedowns on their own balance sheets, which would look bad to their shareholders and investors.

Restructuring that involves exchanging equity for debt means you are actually selling part of your business to raise additional operating capital, hopefully to gain enough time to work out a lasting solution.

An example of how a small business might restructure its debt is a situation in which a business (B) has a very large and critical supplier (S), and the business is also a major customer of this supplier. Falling more and more behind in its payments, B offers to give shares of stock (equity ownership) to S as payment of the debt. B's balance sheet suddenly has significantly fewer liabilities. The bankers are pleased, and it's business as usual—at least for the time being. This is a simplistic example, in large companies, the financial manipulations get pretty complex.

After the many corporate excesses of the 1980s, the pinstripes are out in force. You might say there is a feeding frenzy in progress on the remains of debt-gorged companies. Many large companies are loaded with junk bond financing from takeovers by a larger company or from their own greed to expand too fast and far beyond their ability to pay for the expansion. Numerous recent bankruptcies have involved firms that had been recently "restructured." Unpaid debts of failed businesses totaled $108.8 billion in 1991, a 95.9% increase over 1990.[2]

The legal and accounting fees for both small and larger business restructurings really add up. As an example, in a recent case, Interco (currently in Chapter 11 proceedings) paid over $4 million in fees to Rothschild (a recapitalization specialist) and Morgan Guaranty Bank. While the bankers and restructuring people were getting these enormous fees, the value of Interco bonds dropped from $990 million to around $20 million.[3] In other words, individual bondholders ultimately paid for the restructuring. While the accountants and lawyers prepared Campeau's 6,000 page bankruptcy petition, they earned nearly $4 million in fees plus monthly advisory fees of about $2 million.[4] In a recent article in *Forbes* on the rapidly growing restructuring business, Laura Jereski and Jason Zweig wrote, "What about individual junk bond holders whose insurance money, mutual funds and bank assets are invested in junk? What about employees who are let go or asked to make sacrifices so the companies can pay swollen interest bills and fatten the investment bankers' coffers?"[5] All companies consist of individuals, and how we handle money directly affects people's lives.

Another example of a well-known restructuring that has made all the headlines is the Taj Mahal and the associated Donald Trump holdings. No amount of manipulation can make the reality of a $750-million debt and a $95-million annual interest payment go away. Someone is going to have to absorb tremendous losses: mutual funds, bondholders, investors, banks, and shareholders. Ultimately, at the end of the chain, the individual loses. The current restructuring package will result in an even larger debt, $919 million by the end of the decade—over double the estimated liquidation value of the Taj.[6] The lesson here is to look realistically at the monetary and human gains and losses. Trump's creditors are understandably trying to salvage what they can, short of an actual bankruptcy. However, these financial maneuvers do not really address the internal organizational and management problems that caused the financial difficulties in the first place. The recapitalization of the Taj Mahal will produce an estimated $8 million in fees to the outside people involved in the restructuring. Bondholder advisers' fees often amount to $140,000 per month for large holdings.[7] The Trump empire is a perfect example of how a highly debt-leveraged business very quickly gets into trouble in an economic downturn. The same scenario is repeated over and over again for smaller business firms every time there is a recession or other slump in sales.

Several large insurance companies and major banks were big players in the junk bond financing of the Taj Mahal, as they have been in numerous corporations. When they absorb such staggering losses, there is a dribble effect that eventually reaches down to the small business owner, who then pays higher premiums or receives lower returns on investments or finds it very difficult to obtain legitimate financing for normal business needs.

Insurance companies now own over $66 billion in junk bonds, which accounts for about one third of the total market. The banking industry accounts for another $65 billion of very highly leveraged and often questionable loans.[8] These large creditors, who are very desirous of keeping their balance sheets from looking like a financial disaster from heavy writedowns, are eager for the quick-fix approach so that they can delay or hide from the public the true picture of what is happening. Hence, they will forgo interest on bonds in exchange for equity in a distressed company, switch assets on a balance sheet, or exchange junk bonds for equity, a move that keeps a balance sheet intact and covers up the losses temporarily—until the next crisis.

ADVANTAGES. The obvious advantage is temporary relief from a cash crunch, especially when the restructuring involves exchanging debt for equity. As long as you don't give up control of your business, such an exchange can infuse a large amount of cash into your business without your borrowing it. However, you will have new shareholders, who will certainly be voicing their opinions regarding the operation of your business. There are legitimate reasons to consider restructuring as a partial solution for financial troubles. Restructuring can give a business more time to work out effective solutions to financial problems.

DISADVANTAGES. Restructuring attempts to work with the financial consequences of long-term bad management and failure to make constructive and crucial changes within a company. It's concentrating on the effects without really working on the causes of the financial difficulties. Statistically, very few restructuring efforts do anything other than delay a final day of reckoning, when someone must eventually pay the accumulated bill for past excesses. Restructuring is often a desperate effort to buy time. Ultimately, reality knocks at the executive suite, and the business is either shut down or sold to scavengers for next to nothing.

Frequently, the quick fix is just another delaying tactic on the inevitable slide into financial ruin. You'll hear pure hype masked in exotic terms like *recapitalization, pay-in-kind bonds, principal protectors,* and *turning bonds into equity.* Unfortunately there is no quick fix when it comes to turning around a financially ailing business. It takes old-fashioned hard work, commitment, and careful planning.

TAX CONSEQUENCES. The tax consequences in a debt restructuring are too varied and complex to be included in this book. However, when the debts of a company are converted into equity ownership, deductible interest expenses drop, creating more taxable income, and individual shareholders may find their equity ownership, represented by the stock that they own, highly diluted and worth only a fraction of its original value. The IRS explains that "If a corporation issues its own stock to a creditor in exchange for the cancellation of its debt, the corporation realizes debt cancellation income to the extent that the amount of debt cancelled exceeds the fair market value of the stock."[9] This is a simple view, and most restructurings involve complex tax considerations.

Chapter 13 Plan

There is another alternative to the traditional bankruptcy proceedings; a Chapter 13 plan. However, this is only for individuals and is not allowed for business firms. I mention it here because it is common for personal money troubles to parallel business troubles. Usually the business eventually drains all the owner's personal resources, and the result is double trouble. Consequently, a business bankruptcy or reorganization often triggers an individual bankruptcy or forces the owner of a business also to restructure his or her financial affairs. A Chapter 13 filing can then become a potential alternative for an individual.

The maximum compensation to a trustee under Chapter 13 is 10 percent of all payments allowed. The court commonly sets reasonable fees after a petition is filed and then orders employers to make direct payments to the trustee, who then pays the various creditors. Under a Chapter 13 plan, you take all your debts, add the 10 percent trustee's administration fee, and then divide by 36, 48, or 60 months. This can be a good way to straighten out your personal affairs if you have excess personal debts.

There are two primary tests you can use to decide if you can file a Chapter 13 plan: (1) You must have a regular income or salary, and (2) you must owe less than $100,000 in unsecured debts and less than $350,000 in secured debts. Under certain circumstances, a Chapter 13 case can be converted at any time to a Chapter 7 liquidation.

ADVANTAGES. Creditors are legally prevented from harassing you, provided you continue to make the payments as agreed upon in your repayment plan. You pay back your creditors a reduced amount— sometimes only 20 to 40 percent of the original debt—and at the end of the repayment period, the debts are fully discharged.

A Chapter 13 filing is not a traditional bankruptcy, but a legal reorganization that will free you from creditor harassment and allow you to keep all your assets while you attempt to repay your debts over a three- to five-year period. One requirement is that you must have a salary or wages out of which a payment plan can be worked out; that is to say, you must have sufficient income or wages to file a Chapter 13.

DISADVANTAGES. This plan definitely will have serious consequences for your credit rating! The public views a Chapter 13 as a traditional bankruptcy—probably because of the formal court–trustee handling of the reorganization, and because it is a proceeding in the Bankruptcy Court under the Bankruptcy Code. It looks like a bankruptcy when in reality it is an individual reorganization of one's financial affairs. Credit-reporting agencies report all bankruptcies for ten years, including a Chapter 13 reorganization. This report will cause credit problems for a long time.

Many attorneys and court officials say that most individuals would be better off with a straight bankruptcy—making a clean break and getting a fresh start. This belief stems from statistics that show that about 80 percent of the individuals who undertake Chapter 13 plans never complete their repayments and eventually end up in a straight bankruptcy. Court administrative expenses will cost you from 10 to 20 percent, deducted from the payments the court makes to creditors.[10] You may be prevented from filing a straight bankruptcy (Chapter 7 liquidation) for six years if you file a Chapter 13 repayment.

TAX CONSEQUENCES. A Chapter 13 reorganization will not exempt you from paying your income taxes—past, present, or future. Income from cancellation of debt is *not* taxable, but "tax attribute" rules may result in reducing certain other tax deductions. You may lose certain interest deductions from the suspension of interest charges that is required by law under this plan. Of course, you continue to pay all taxes as usual: wage withholding, real estate and property taxes, and so on.

Should You Sell Your Business?

Selling your business (or a part of it) is an alternative to bankruptcy, although you should do your best to avoid a *distress* sale. To get the best price for your business, it will be to your advantage to straighten out any financial problems as much as possible before attempting a sale. The reasons for selling your business or a share of it usually include one or several of the following:

- *The need for additional operating capital.* This is a very common occurrence when a business expands too rapidly and is unable to finance receivables and inventory. Over-expansion is a major cause of business failures. Many firms are forced to close for this reason.
- *The need for greater expertise in the operation of your business.* This need can be accomplished by selling a share either through the sale of stock or by letting in a partner. A competent partner with cash to invest and helpful experience in your particular business may be a perfect remedy to a multitude of problems. Sometimes the only way to save a business is to bring in entirely new owners with the particular talents and abilities needed in your business.
- Selling your business may enable you to get a better price now as opposed to waiting for further financial deterioration. If you are not up to the task of reorganization, it is better to cut your losses than to hang onto a sinking ship and eventually lose everything.
- You don't like the business you are in and want out. If you find yourself in the wrong work and can't see yourself continuing, then you might as well sell out and get into another line of work. However, it may require some reorganization efforts on your part to get your business into financial shape before a sale is possible or advisable.

Before considering the sale of your business, you will need to determine its approximate value. A realistic business valuation not only will make it clear if a sale is an actual possibility but will help point out the weak and strong areas in your company. If your business valuation shows a negative net worth, you may find it impossible to give it away. There are many approaches to placing a value on a business. Also, certain methods commonly used in certain industries, such as real estate, calculate a property as selling for a certain multiple of the net income produced. Other businesses arrive at values based on percentages of existing and future contracts or billings.

PREPARING YOUR BUSINESS VALUATION. The best method I have come across is called the *stabilized-income approach*. This method works well for most businesses and has the added advantage of getting you to see your business from the buyer's point of view. Here is how you prepare your business valuation based on the stabilized-income method:[11]

Step 1. Set Up a Stabilized Income Statement. You begin with the most recent income statement and adjust this statement to eliminate items that are distorted because of accounting methods or special fringe benefits that are not normal operating expenses. The goal is to establish the *real* earning power of your business. This is definitely not a way to hide problems in your business from a potential buyer or investor but a way to accurately and objectively reflect the actual income and profit that can be expected over the next twelve months under normal conditions.

You should carefully put in writing detailed explanations of each adjustment so that, in the event of serious interest, it will be perfectly clear to a buyer what you have done.

In Exhibit 1.1, an example of a stabilized-income statement is compared with the actual income statement as prepared by an accountant. The notes at the bottom of the example explain the adjustments to the actual income statement.

Other minor adjustments are made through a detailed analysis of each expense category. In the stabilized-income approach, interest expense is *not* included because it is an expense item that varies widely depending on the financial structure of a company under a particular owner. A *cost-of-ownership calculation* is done later in the valuation process that compensates for this.

Typical adjustments include replacing the owner's salary with a salary that accurately reflects what it would cost the company to hire a replacement for the present owner, for instance, a paid manager with the necessary expertise to operate the business. Depreciation expense is also replaced with an item called *replacement fund*. This is an expense that gives an indication of how much should be set aside regularly (as in a savings account) to replace worn-out equipment.

Step 2. Determine the Value of Tangible Assets. In this step, you estimate (hire a professional appraiser if needed) the value of all your

Stabilized Income Statement

Income Statement	Actual 1992	%	Stabilized: 12 Months	%
(1) Sales Revenue	$650,000.00	100.0	$700,000.00	100.0
(2) Cost of Goods Sold	197,600.00	30.4	212,800.00	30.4
(2) Labor Costs	187,200.00	28.8	201,600.00	28.8
Gross Profit	265,200.00	40.8	285,600.00	40.8
Selling Expense	86,750.00	13.4	92,400.00	13.2
Administrative Expenses	52,650.00	8.1	42,000.00	6.0
(3) Owner's Salary	40,000.00	6.2	49,000.00	7.0
(4) Replacement Fund or Depreciation	11,700.00	1.8	21,000.00	3.0
Maintenance & Repairs	5,200.00	0.8	7,000.00	1.0
Miscellaneous	5,200.00	0.8	7,000.00	1.0
Total Expenses	201,500.00	31.0	218,400.00	31.2
Net Profit Before Taxes	$63,700.00	9.8	$67,200.00	9.6

Assumptions:
1. Sales will increase at inflation rate assumed to be 7.7%.
2. Operating costs will remain at constant percentages.
3. Owner's salary should be increased by $9,000 to reflect current pay rates offered in comparable businesses.
4. A $21,000 replacement fund will be substituted for depreciation expense. This will be used to replace equipment as needed.

EXHIBIT 1.1

tangible assets, such as land, buildings, equipment, vehicles, and inventory—everything needed to operate your business. Exhibit 1.2 is an example of the asset value for our hypothetical company. Note that our example includes working capital as an obvious asset in the normal operations of the business.

Asset Values

Land	$20,000.00
Buildings	120,000.00
Inventory	60,000.00
Equipment	60,000.00
Working Capital Needed	40,000.00
Total Assets	**$300,000.00**

EXHIBIT 1.2

Cost of Money	
Value of Tangible Assets	$300,000.00
Underlying Interest Rate	12%
Cost of Money (.12 x $300,000)	$36,000.00

EXHIBIT 1.3

Step 3. Determine the Cost of Money. This is a specialized calculation that estimates the cost of owning the tangible assets itemized in Step 2. This is a substitute for the interest expense category that we omitted from our stabilized-income statement. To keep our interest rate a more stable number than the bank prime rate, we base it on the current inflation rate, adding 4 percentage points. Thus, in our example, we set this rate at 12 percent (7.7 percent in Exhibit 1.1 plus 4 percent). The cost of money applies only to the tangible assets for our business as determined in Step 2. Exhibit 1.3 shows you how to make this calculation.

Step 4. Determine Excess Earnings Amount. You calculate excess earnings to see how much your business earns as net profit after the cost of money is subtracted from the stabilized profit (Exhibit 1.1). You then determine the excess earnings as shown in Exhibit 1.4.

Step 5. Calculate a Multiple for Excess Earnings. This multiple is a number that gives you a way to rank the business as to risk, stability, desirability, and other factors that affect the value of the excess earnings ($31,200) that were calculated in Step 4. Step 5 is important because it gives you a measure of how a prospective buyer will judge the general quality of your business. Exhibit 1.5 details the steps in determining the excess earnings multiple.

Excess Earnings	
Stabilized Profit	$67,200.00
(From Exhibit 1.1)	
Cost of Money	-36,000.00
(From Exhibit 1.3)	
Excess Earnings	**$31,200.00**

EXHIBIT 1.4

Calculating the Excess Earnings Multiple

Risk Rating (from 0 to 6):

> 0 = Continuity of income is at risk
> 3 = Steady income is likely
> 6 = Growing income is assured

Competitive Rating (from 0 to 6):

> 0 = Highly competitive in unstable market conditions
> 3 = Normal competitive conditions
> 6 = Very little competition in market and high entry cost for new competition

Industry Rating (from 0 to 6):

> 0 = A declining industry
> 3 = Industry growth somewhat faster than inflation
> 6 = A dynamic industry with rapid growth reasonably certain

Company Rating (from 0 to 6):

> 0 = A recent start-up, not yet established
> 3 = Well established with a good track record
> 6 = Long record of sound operations with solid reputation

Company Growth Rating (from 0 to 6):

> 0 = Business has been declining
> 3 = Steady growth, slightly faster than inflation
> 6 = Dynamic growth rate

Desirability Rating (from 0 to 6):

> 0 = Not status, rough or dirty work
> 3 = Respected business in satisfactory environment
> 6 = Challenging business in an attractive environment

Rating Formula:

> 4.0 = Risk Rating
> 3.0 = Competitive Rating
> 3.5 = Industry Rating
> 5.0 = Company Rating
> 4.0 = Company Growth Rating
> 4.0 = Desirability Rating
> --
> 23.5 = Total Rating Points
> **3.9 = Multiple (total rating points divided by 6)**

EXHIBIT 1.5

Step 6. Calculate Excess Earnings Value. In Exhibit 1.6, the multiple we determined in Step 5 is now used to calculate the monetary value of the excess earnings.

Value of Excess Earnings	
Excess Earnings (from Ex. 1.4)	$31,200.00
Multiple (from Ex. 1.5) x	3.9
Value of Excess Earnings	**$121,680.00**

EXHIBIT 1.6

Step 7. Determine the Total Business Value. The final step (Exhibit 1.7) is to find the total value of the business. This is accompanied by adding the value of the excess earnings ($121,680) to the value of the total tangible assets (Exhibit 1.2).

This method for obtaining the market value of a business is an excellent way to arrive at a realistic price, provided each step is carefully and objectively worked out. The evaluation process detailed in Step 5 adds a premium, a type of goodwill, to the value of the business if warranted. It is not uncommon for a business to end up with a negative amount of excess earnings. In this case, the business is not even worth the value of its tangible assets.

WHEN YOU SHOULD NOT USE THIS APPROACH. In practice, every business is unique, and although the stabilized-income method is an excellent approach, occasionally it may not work and should not be used. Major exceptions are

- *Hi-tech businesses.* These are generally valued by market conditions and may vary widely in price.
- *Information businesses.* These are very difficult to value and are often sold based on future sales and earnings.
- *Hobby businesses.* These types of businesses are part fun and part business and are sold to different types of buyers. Their value is often subjective and difficult to determine.

Total Business Value	
*Value of Assets	$260,000.00
Value of Excess Earnings	+ $121,680.00
Total Business Value	**$381,680.00**

Note: The $40,000 working capital added to the assets in Exhibit 1.2 is not used here. A new owner must add this to the purchase price of the business.

EXHIBIT 1.7

- *High-leverage businesses.* Such businesses have special qualities that make this method ineffective. This type of business may have exclusive rights or licenses or, as in real estate, may be sold based on industry formulas.
- *Professional businesses.* Medical, accounting, and legal practices and other professional businesses usually have industry guidelines that decide selling prices.
- *Start-ups.* Here the difficulty is obvious: The lack of a track record and many unknown factors make an accurate valuation very difficult.

HOW THE TERMS OF A SALE AFFECT THE PRICE. The actual price that is paid for a business commonly varies from its value as determined in a valuation. The reason is that the terms of a sale have a strong influence on the sale price. As an example, if current interest rates are quite low and the seller is willing to carry extended terms with a relatively small down payment, then a higher price can be obtained. Using a carefully worked out method such as this will make it much easier to convince a buyer of the value of your business.

SELLING A PART OF YOUR BUSINESS. Should you want to take in a partner or investor, you will need to find a current market value for your business, and the stabilized-income method is one of the best approaches because it takes into consideration the economic climate and approaches the valuation from the perspective of a prospective buyer or investor. Keep in mind that you should be absolutely sure a prospective partner or investor is compatible with you and your employees. You can choose many alternatives depending on what is best for your particular circumstances. You may want an active working partner or a silent partner, or simply outside investors. The role of a partner or investor should be clarified in a partnership or shareholders agreement prepared by a lawyer.

You may be able to sell stock to your employees or to certain key employees. It may be in your best interest to take in one or several key employees as partners, especially if their expertise is crucial to the ongoing success of your business. When you consider selling a part of your company, you need to decide how much control you are willing to give up. Shareholders in a corporation, even though holding a minority interest, may still cause substantial difficulty if they take adversarial views of how you are operating your business.

Advantages. Selling your business (all or part) is a viable alternative to bankruptcy. However, if your financial affairs have deteriorated too far, you may find it difficult or impossible to sell your business, or to extricate yourself from your financial entanglements unless you first reorganize your business affairs. Additional advantages are:

- Selling all or a portion of your business can quickly straighten out financial difficulties by adding more operating capital.
- New owners or investors often bring fresh ideas, experience, and talent that will help in revitalizing your business.
- Selling now may be a better option than a slow financial death, if you find yourself in an impossible situation.
- A sale of your business can give you a fresh start in a new or different business.

Disadvantages. The number one disadvantage is that you lose your business, probably at a distressed price if you are having any financial difficulties. You will have to discount your price enough to offset the negative financial numbers. In many cases, this means you may sell your business and walk away with little or nothing but paperwork to show for your effort and hard work. Depending on your situation and skills, you may find yourself joining the ranks of the unemployed. Selling may be an easy way out, but you might seriously regret the decision later—that you didn't make a real effort to save your business, or at least to try.

I know of one situation in which a profitable business was sold and part of the sale included a large note with substantial monthly payments to the former owner. A few months after the sale, the new owner filed bankruptcy, dissolved the company, and never made another payment to the former owner. Later, it was discovered that this buyer had purchased numerous companies, milking their assets and then filing bankruptcy—it was a racket. The lesson is obvious. Before you sell your business to anyone, it is well worth the extra cost to have her or his background checked to make sure you are dealing with a reputable and legitimate buyer.

Tax Consequences. Selling your business definitely calls for expert help from your accountant or a tax expert in business transactions. There are ways to spread out taxable income, such as installment purchase contracts, so that you do not end up with a huge tax bite at the time of the sale. Or you may find yourself with substantial losses and no way to take advantage of them on your personal tax return because of the current restrictions on capital losses ($1,500 for an individual) that you can deduct each year and alternative minimum tax laws.

Whether your business is a corporation, a sole proprietorship, or a partnership changes the tax treatment when it is sold. When you sell a sole proprietorship, you are usually selling many different types of assets that are each treated differently by the IRS. Basically, you will have gains or losses depending on the particular asset. Ownership in a corporation is represented by shares of stock. As a result, when you sell your stock, you will have a capital gain or a capital loss, depending on your cost in relationship to the selling price. A corporation can sell its business assets and then close the corporation. In a partnership or joint venture, each partner's interest is treated as a capital asset when sold. Any other gains or losses from unrealized receivables or inventory are treated as ordinary gains or losses.

Self-Reorganization

Albert Einstein said, "In the middle of difficulty lies opportunity." Self-reorganization is the best choice if you want to save your business and you are willing to make the effort. You negotiate on an individual basis with each creditor, stop all legal or collection threats, create new cash flow for your business, pay each debt, and give yourself valuable time and space to reorganize and rethink your affairs. In this book, we also examine the most critical aspect of business operations, keeping in mind that people are a company's most vital asset or liability; that is, problems or solutions do not exist on their own but are an inseparable part of human relations. Self-reorganization is the method I will proceed to explain in detail in the following chapters.

ADVANTAGES. A well-planned and properly implemented self-reorganization not only has the potential to cure business financial ills but can also revitalize and rejuvenate all aspects of your business, giving it new life and a promising future. A self-reorganization gives you the maximum benefit at the minimum cost and frequently enables you to avoid or minimize attorneys' fees in the process. This method will earn you the respect and confidence of your creditors and maintain your integrity and reputation in the business community. You will be saving jobs for your employees and quite possibly even creating more jobs in the future.

DISADVANTAGES. It is difficult to see any disadvantages in this approach. However, there is one drawback that seems obvious, and that is that you may undertake the considerable effort required in a self-reorganization and then still end up losing your business in bankruptcy proceedings. Even taking into consideration the potential event of bankruptcy, I know your self-esteem will be very much more intact and you will be at peace with your conscience for making the effort.

TAX CONSEQUENCES. In a self-reorganization, most tax consequences involve possible losses sustained from the sale of various assets or excess inventory at reduced prices in the process of getting your company into a more liquid cash position. If your business has been sustaining losses for several years, you can certainly use those losses to reduce taxes on future profits. In a turnaround situation, the old losses become valuable assets that will give you some temporary tax relief.

Minimizing Debt

There are many reasons for financial difficulties in a business. However, debt is always a major contributing villain in a crisis. When you have principal and interest payments to meet, even a small recession or slump in the economy can mean the end.

We are conditioned to believe that debt is normal in the operation of a business. We are told it is foolish not to use the leverage made possible through borrowing. In fact, debt adds a significant risk to the operation of any business enterprise. Going into debt is often the result of financial pressure, impatience, greed, or simply not knowing the alternative ways to start a business or to finance expansion. Numerous successful businesses of all sizes operate with no debt at all and do not consider debt a solution in any business circumstance. Borrowing money means you have taken in a not-so-silent partner who will often dictate to you how to operate your business in addition to draining off your profits through excessive interest charges. It is a parasitical relationship. These additional expenses can easily make it more difficult for a business to stay competitive, especially in hard times. If a competent individual has a valid business idea that provides a needed product or service and has no funds or savings, it should be possible, with proper planning and effort, to raise capital for the venture by selling stock or partnership shares or by finding investors in the enterprise. There are thousands of stories of how individuals started on a small scale and then grew rapidly. One such example is Gateway Computers, which began in a barn with two friends assembling computer parts and selling them with small mail-order ads. Gateway is now a multimillion-dollar firm employing about 1,400 persons.

Businesses, like individuals, have been brainwashed for decades by slick Madison Avenue advertising campaigns designed to get us to accept the notion that going into debt is not only OK but smart! Everywhere we see and hear ads with some friendly banker helping a business to expand. Prudent borrowing in special situations may sometimes be necessary. However, successful businesses are not influenced by social pressure to borrow money.

Don't borrow any more money if at all possible! In a time of financial difficulty, there is the very strong impulse to keep borrowing to help pay other loans. Whatever you do, resist this impulse. Continued borrowing is just postponing the day of reckoning and makes the situation even more difficult. The lesson in any financial crisis involving debts is not to add to your existing debt. A debt often becomes a burden that outweighs any benefits obtained. To keep your peace of mind, pay as you go, and resolve to stay out of debt in your business and in your personal life. You'll sleep better, and when difficult economic times come, as they always do, you'll have a much better chance of survival.

If you owe money to anyone, you have a debt. As a matter of clarification, when I refer to debt in a business, I mean bank, auto, equipment, or other financing arrangements. I do not mean normal thirty-day trade credit extended by suppliers as a convenience in paying bills at the end of the month. However, amounts owed beyond the customary thirty-day period are considered an unnecessary indebtedness to a particular creditor, as well as a sign of probable financial difficulties. Insolvency is commonly defined as the condition in which a business can no longer pay its normal operating expenses on time. However, bankruptcy law states that the condition of insolvency exists when debts and liabilities exceed the value of all assets.

Debt: How Much Is Too Much?

By the 1990s, the average U.S. company was spending 50 percent of its pretax earnings on interest payments, compared with 32 percent in 1980.[12] There are many legitimate needs for additional funds in a new or growing business. However, borrowing money should be a last resort, to be considered only after all other possibilities have been exhausted, such as the sale of stock (equity financing), taking in a partner or partners, or finding venture capital.

Any debt can be too much. If your company is not generating several times the principal and interest payments in added net profits directly attributable to the use of the borrowed funds, you have too much debt. Too much debt places your business future—and consequently your future and the future of your employees—at great risk. Banks judge a company's basic financial health by determining the ratio of current assets to current liabilities (liabilities due within one year or less). Any number below a 1-to-1 ratio is considered a danger signal and may mean excess liabilities in relation to a company's ability to pay.

The recent trend is a mushrooming corporate debt load that is having devastating effects on the economy on a world, national, and individual basis. Statistics show American corporations with over $2 trillion of debt. The corporate debt is growing rapidly, at a rate greater than the increase in net worth. In fact, corporate debt now exceeds net worth by over 12 percent and absorbs over *50 percent* of corporate cash flow.[13] This staggering amount of money used to service debt is frightening when we consider how disastrous even a small downturn in the economy can be for highly leveraged companies. We are now seeing daily news reports about the consequences of this flagrant abuse of debt in the form of failing companies and massive layoffs and cutbacks.

Checklist Points

1. Begin now to minimize or eliminate all borrowing. Do not add to any bank or other loans if at all possible.
2. Be sure that you have carefully considered all the alternatives and that you feel right about your choice. A confident and determined attitude on your part will influence others and will be a valuable asset in your reorganization plans.
3. Make a preliminary evaluation of assets, debts, and relations with customers, creditors, and employees. Do this with the intent to get a more precise idea of the specific problem areas that need priority treatment or special attention and effort.
4. Also, now is a good time to touch base with your accountant and your attorney. Let them know about your plans. They may have some helpful advice and suggestions that you didn't consider. Keeping them informed about what is going on will enable them to quickly assist you in the event of some emergency situation. But keep them in the background for now. You want to minimize legal and accounting expenses as much as possible.

You will find that many methods presented in the following chapters also work well for an individual and can be easily adapted to straighten out one's personal finances without filing any kind of bankruptcy. Well, it's onward and upward! With our determination set, we will now tackle the nitty-gritty, nuts-and-bolts, do-it-now adventure of saving your business, keeping in mind Winston Churchill's advice, "Never, never, never, never give up."

2

Damage Control

Quick Steps to Buy Time

I have discovered the Philosopher's stone which turns everything into gold; it is "Pay as you go."
—Folk Saying

Step 1: Assessing Your Current Situation

Delay and procrastination can be fatal. If you do nothing concrete to change your circumstances, you are quickly going to be another statistic in the ever-mounting numbers of business failures. Will Rogers said, "Even if you're on the right track you'll get run over if you just sit there." There is a story:

> The four-engine plane was having engine troubles. The flight attendant's voice crackled over the speaker system: "We are having some problems with one of our engines, but there is no real danger. We will be slightly delayed, about thirty minutes, using only three engines." Many passengers were concerned, but Art Slothby, a passenger on his way to a seminar on how to get rich in real estate without any money, reassured his fellow travelers, "Thirty minutes isn't so bad. Life will go on. After all it is just one engine."
>
> Some time passed and again the flight attendant's voice announced: "I am sorry to announce that our number two engine is having some problems, but there is nothing to worry about. We will be about sixty minutes late flying on our other two engines." This time the passengers were quite alarmed, but Slothby again reassured them, saying: "Let's not make a big deal about one hour. We're still way ahead of ground travel, and we have two good engines to get us there." Everybody calmed down once more.

After some time passed, the flight attendant announced over the speaker system: "We have some bad news. A third engine is having fuel line problems and we will be two hours late arriving." Slothby remarked, "I only hope the number four engine doesn't have any problems, or we'll all be up here all day!"[1]

Unresolved problems are not going to disappear, they will only get worse as time goes on, and as our friend Slothby learned, what begins as a little problem can quickly prove fatal. If your business is in financial difficulty, you most likely have some creditors pressing you for payment. Our first priority is to remove this pressure so that you can concentrate on your own reorganization plans.

In order to avoid unnecessary problems, be careful to pay all payroll taxes, bank loans, and lease and rental payments on time. The IRS can very quickly seize your assets or money in your bank account. Payroll taxes do not belong to you and you should never consider using any of these funds. I recommend that you pay all payroll taxes immediately. Most outside payroll services can arrange to pay all federal and state taxes through electronic fund transfers on each pay date. This way you are always current. State and federal tax departments are unlikely to negotiate anything with you. They are quite likely to severely disrupt or shut down your business if you don't keep all payroll taxes current.

You may need your bank as a future credit reference. At this stage in your reorganization, you do not want to alarm your bank by missing any loan payments. Later on, you may decide to negotiate new loan terms. Be careful to remain in good standing with your landlord in the event you need to renegotiate a new lease or to sublet your present property.

Your Critical Path

I want to give you an overview of the reorganization steps in a time-sequenced order of events. This is your personal "razor's edge," or the path you must walk to turn around your business operations. It gives you a much simplified, but clear, picture of the overall process involved. Modify the following example to set up your own critical path. Establish target dates for the completion of each aspect of your reorganization.

BUSINESS REORGANIZATION: CRITICAL PATH

Phase I. Stop Creditor Harassment
    A. Prepare cash flow report (before reorganization)
        1. Establish your minimum cash flow needs.
        2. Determine the total of deferred cash payments to creditors
    B. Set up detailed creditor repayment plan
        1. Open backup vendor accounts (optional)
        2. Get needed legal forms if any
    C. Prepare a revised cash flow report (after accounts payable deferrals)
    D. Send letters to selected creditors
    E. Establish backup bank (optional)

Phase II. Reorganize Operations
    A. Personnel
        1. Set up organization chart
        2. Establish proper chain of command
        3. Review employee management, compensation, motivation
        4. Make necessary changes: hours, benefits, layoffs, etc.
    B. Implement proper internal control procedures
        1. Initiating and approving transactions
        2. Checking custody of business assets
        3. Keeping records
    C. Enforce accounts receivable policies and terms
        1. Put slow payers on COD
        2. Set up system to collect past-due accounts
        3. Check credit before all shipments
        4. Set up accounts receivable aging follow-up and report system
        5. Screen all new accounts
    D. Establish control over all purchasing.
    E. Set up necessary inventory control procedures, and sell or liquidate excess
    F. Review pricing, advertising, and marketing
    G. Check each expense category for ways to save money, and eliminate nonessentials

Phase III. Monitor and Verify Results: Establish a Verification System
- A. Initiate daily and weekly status reports
- B. Meet with staff
- C. Form problem-solving groups
- D. Report on cash flow
- E. Report on cash flow budget variance
- F. Compile monthly comparative financial statements
- G. Determine break-even point
- H. Set up monitoring schedule for vital statistics

Preparing Your Cash Flow Analysis

Exhibit 2.1 is a sample monthly cash-flow analysis. You need to complete one to see exactly what your present situation is and how much you need to trim monthly expenses to continue operating. First, for an average month, list your total cash receipts (estimated) from all sources. To get more accurate results, average at least a six-month period for items that vary in amount each month. Keep in mind that this is a cash flow analysis, so do not include any accounts receivable other than what you expect to receive as cash payments during a typical month.

Next, list your expected monthly expenses. Purchases for resale would include all suppliers of goods or services that you sell to others. As an example, a restaurant would include all purchases of food, liquor, and beverages during an average month. A contractor would include all job-site labor, materials, and subcontractors as purchases for resale. Average your actual purchases over the last three to six months. Then divide this total by the average monthly sales for the same period to get an average percentage of sales for purchases each month. In our example, Able Company's average monthly purchases total $40,608, about 51 percent of the $79,000 sales revenue.

You can estimate how much your monthly purchases should total by using information from your financial statements. Able Company's recent financial statements show a gross profit of 60 percent, resulting in a cost of goods sold of 40 percent. We can see that Able Company's purchases are excessive—causing increased inventory investment and lower turnover, a real drain on cash. For example, sales of $79,000 with an average gross profit of 60 percent would

ABLE COMPANY MONTHLY CASH FLOW ANALYSIS		
CASH RECEIPTS		$79,000
MONTHLY EXPENSES:		
Purchases for Resale (51.4%)	$40,608	
Rent: Building & Equipment	5,500	
Salaries	20,890	
Executive Salaries	4,500	
Payroll Taxes	3,047	
Fringe Benefits	1,282	
Accounting & Legal	1,200	
Advertising	1,600	
Office Supplies & Postage	195	
Insurance	1,250	
Utilities	750	
Operating Supplies	5,172	
Telephone	694	
Auto Expense	688	
Miscellaneous	176	
Bank Loan (Principal)	1,667	
Bank Loan (Interest)	830	
Other Loans	429	
TOTAL MONTHLY EXPENSE		$90,478
CASH FLOW FOR MONTH		($11,478)

EXHIBIT 2.1

give you a purchase cost of (100 percent−60 percent) = 40 percent × $79,000, or $31,600. Able Company's purchases should average about $32,000 each month at their present sales level of $79,000. A simple way to calculate your gross profit percentage is to subtract the cost from the selling price of your product. This result gives you your profit. Divide the profit by the selling price, and you will get the gross profit percentage as a result.

Complete each expense category, being as realistic and as accurate as possible with your figures. Payroll taxes consist of your company's share of FICA taxes and unemployment taxes. For bank loans, list the principal and interest payments separately. Total your monthly expenses and subtract this amount from the total cash receipts. This is your cash flow under your present circumstances. Your cash flow, negative or positive, is a very important number because it gives you a target amount to use as a guideline in restructuring your business finances.

Able Company (Exhibit 2.1) has a negative cash flow. It is losing about $11,478 each month. It needs to eliminate a minimum of $11,500 in cash outflows just to break even.

Creating Cash Without Borrowing: Your Repayment Plan

Your next step is to determine a repayment plan for those creditors whom you are late paying or are unable to pay at all. This is an extremely important step. Not only will it remove the pressure of calls about past-due accounts from suppliers, but it will also help to eliminate potential lawsuits. This step provides operating cash and valuable time to work out a solution for your business, and you should give it number one priority!

First list all of your accounts payable (only open and unpaid bills) for the month. We are going to defer seven of the larger accounts in Able Company's list of creditors. In Exhibit 2.2, Able Company's creditors are listed. Our goal will be to defer the maximum amount possible in order to give us a good safety cushion and time to reorganize operations.

Following the example (Exhibit 2.2), list the total amount owed to each creditor, the amount past due, and the number of days past due. The more you are able to defer, the more time and space you will create to reorganize your business affairs. Now divide the total amount owed by the maximum number of payments you feel each particular supplier will be willing to accept. Keep in mind it does not hurt to try for more payments. You may have to negotiate a little occasionally to get a final agreement. You'll usually find that the creditor will accept your first offer provided it is properly presented as explained later. Some creditors may want to charge interest on the past-due portion. Try to avoid interest charges, but pay the interest charges if they become a stumbling block in your negotiations. Your most important goal is to stretch out payments as much as possible. "Cash Flow Created" (the last column) is the difference between the proposed monthly payment and the total amount owed. As you can see from Exhibit 2.2, we have deferred $81,099 of accounts payable. Our first month's payments total only $7,660.

			DAYS	NEW	NO	Deferred Pmts
CREDITOR	TOTAL OWED	AMOUNT PAST DUE	PAST DUE	MONTHLY PAYMENT	OF PMTS	CASH FLOW CREATED
Company A	$52,483	$40,080	120	$4,374	12	$48,109
Company B	1,254	938	120	209	6	1,045
Company C	16,500	12,375	120	1,375	12	15,125
Company D	5,598	4,200	120	467	12	5,131
Company E	1,902	1,520	150	211	9	1,691
Company F	3,798	2,533	90	422	9	3,376
Company G	7,224	5,415	120	602	12	6,622
TOTALS	$88,759	$67,061		$7,660		$81,099

CREDITOR REPAYMENT PLAN

EXHIBIT 2.2

SOME IMPORTANT PRECAUTIONS

1. Be very careful not to offer any payment terms that you will be unable to meet. Again, you should try for the maximum possible terms with enough creditors so that you gain the maximum time possible to restructure your affairs.
2. Consider opening accounts with additional, backup suppliers, especially for critical items. Take care of this before beginning negotiations with your creditors.
3. Keep three of your vendors paid perfectly to use as credit references when necessary.
4. Negotiate with suppliers for better prices. If you are paying cash, ask for at least a 2 to 5 percent cash discount.

PREPARING A REVISED CASH FLOW BUDGET. In our example for Able Company, the revised cash flow (Exhibit 2.3) is the same except for beginning cash, payments to vendors (old bills), and purchases not deferred. The beginning cash is the ($11,478) negative cash flow that Able Company ended up with after subtracting expenses from receipts. Now, instead of trying to pay last month's purchases plus the past due amounts, Able Company pays only $9,170—the total planned monthly payment to vendors plus a small amount for purchases that were not deferred (Exhibit 2.2).

The purchases not deferred are $1,510. This amount assumes that Able Company is now going to purchase only the goods needed to

ABLE COMPANY REVISED MONTHLY CASH FLOW ANALYSIS		
BEGINNING CASH		($11,478)
CASH RECEIPTS		$79,000
TOTAL CASH AVAILABLE		$67,522
MONTHLY EXPENSES:		
Payments to Vendors (Repayment Plan)	$7,660	
Purchases Not Deferred	1,510	
Rent: Building & Equipment	5,500	
Salaries	20,890	
Executive Salaries	4,500	
Payroll Taxes	3,047	
Fringe Benefits	1,282	
Accounting & Legal	1,200	
Advertising	1,600	
Office Supplies & Postage	195	
Insurance	1,250	
Utilities	750	
Operating Supplies	5,172	
Telephone	694	
Auto Expense	688	
Miscellaneous	176	
Bank Loan (Principal)	1,667	
Bank Loan (Interest)	830	
Other Loans	429	
TOTAL MONTHLY EXPENSE		$59,040
CASH FLOW FOR MONTH		$19,960
ENDING CASH		$8,482

EXHIBIT 2.3

fill orders, being careful not to add to the present inventory unless it is unavoidable. Then, we add the estimated cash receipts of $79,000 to the ($11,478) beginning cash to get a total cash available of $67,522. Next, we enter the same amounts for each expense category from our first cash flow analysis (Exhibit 2.1). This leaves a substantial $19,960 cash flow *without reducing any other expenses*. Remember, now you must purchase only the items needed to fill orders and *only* when you have the order in hand.

Instead of paying over $40,000 for current purchases plus trying to pay some part of the past-due bills, Able Company pays only $9,170, creating a positive cash flow of $19,960—a considerable cash infusion for Able Company. The loss of $11,478 is eliminated!

As quoted in *Changing Times* (Jan. '91), Tom Hufford, director of the Indiana Consumer Credit Counseling Service, said, "Creditors will fall off their chairs if you contact them first. They have a lot of latitude early on to temporarily waive or reduce payments."

Step 2. Notifying Creditors

Each letter (see Exhibit 2.4) should be worded very carefully to present an offer that is not really negotiable but is an improvement in the existing situation for the creditor. The letters we send (Exhibit 2.4) to each creditor will be timed to arrive at the time of the month when we would normally pay for the entire month's purchases.

Offer the creditor a definite repayment schedule and also offer to pay cash for current purchases until the past-due portion is paid in full. It may not be necessary to do this with every supplier, but consider this approach for any supplier you are behind in paying, especially if the amount owed is large. This method accomplishes three very important objectives: (1) you gradually pay off old accounts; (2) you do not add to any existing debt with current purchases; and (3) you gain time to reorganize your affairs.

Carefully note the wording of the sample letter in Exhibit 2.4. Try to follow this format as much as possible in your letters. Keep in mind that you do not want to alarm any of your suppliers by your letter. Instead, you want to reassure them that they are going to be paid and that you are going to remain in business. You should not go into any details about your financial difficulties with any supplier.

Documenting Your Agreements and Payments

Be sure to send your first payment along with the letter. Your payment will help convince the creditor of your sincerity and strengthen the chances for acceptance of your first offer. You may want to consider sending all the payments due on the account as a series of post-dated checks. Often, this action will convince a particularly suspicious creditor that you are serious.

Again, be sure you get all details of your agreed-upon payments in writing with signed copies for your files. It does not hurt to have documents witnessed. However, this is not critical. Be sure

---

ABLE COMPANY
1200 Profit Ave.
Yourtown, Colorado 80210

4/12/92

Attn: Credit Department
Western Supply Co.
7715 Peakview Road
Denver, Colorado 80203

Re: Account #8604:

We apologize for our past-due account with your firm.

Our company has experienced a temporary shortage of operating capital, and we are in the process of reorganizing certain aspects of our business.

My records indicate a current balance owed of $16,500. In order to immediately begin reducing the past-due portion of our account, I have enclosed a payment of $1,375. We will send you eleven additional monthly payments in the same amount, thus paying the above balance in full.

With your approval, we would like to continue to purchase on a cash basis until our account is current.

Thanks for your patience in this matter!

Sincerely,

David C. Able
President

Encl: Check #1204 of 4/12/92 for $1,375

EXHIBIT 2.4

to keep all canceled checks when returned by your bank, as they are actually minicontracts. Cashing your first check is an act of acceptance of your plan, but only if the check clearly links the payment with the terms of the letter. On the front of the check write: "Payment made per terms of cover letter dated 4/12/92." Remember to keep copies of your payment checks and letters before you mail them.

Keep a record of the payments you make to each company. The simplest method is to use a columnar pad with a description space and three or four columns to keep track of the dates, the payment amounts, and the balance as it is paid down, or you can set up a very simple spreadsheet on your PC for your record keeping.

Filling Out Your Own Legal Forms

In Appendix B, you'll find sample legal forms such as an agreement to extend debt payment and extension agreements. You may encounter a creditor who will insist on some form of written agreement other than your letter. This is OK, and it protects you from creditors' changing their minds and suddenly demanding more money or different terms. If this happens, you can use a suitable form from one of the examples. Be sure you keep a signed copy for your files.

As an option, you can attach two copies of the agreement to extend debt payment to your letter for the creditor to sign. Each copy should be marked "One of two duplicate originals." Be sure to fill out the terms clearly and sign both copies. One copy will be for the creditor's records, and the other is to be returned for your records. Normally, a copy of a signed original is sufficient legally if you know where the original is. If you decide to use this approach, just add a brief explanation at the end of the sample letter asking the creditor to sign and return the extension agreement. It has been my experience that in 99 percent of the cases, this will not be necessary, and your letter of intent with the first payment attached will prove to be sufficient.

If possible, *do not* sign any promissory notes at this point in your plan. A signed note places you in an unflexible position and enables a creditor to begin collection procedures very quickly if you default on your agreed-upon payment terms. Sometimes creditors will want you to sign a note for the amount of the indebtedness. However, you should avoid doing so if possible and stick to your letter of intent and your repayment plan.

You do not have to have your lawyer call a creditor's lawyer to settle matters. You should first try calling the creditor's lawyer yourself. It is often easy to work out an agreement. I know of one situation in which a $1,000 debt was settled in this way for only $10 per month with a simple phone call. Most people are more than willing to work out an agreement. Trouble is automatic when there is no communication.

How to Handle Verbal Agreements

If your initial agreement with a creditor is verbal, you should immediately send a confirming letter to the creditor. I do not recommend that you use the phone to initiate your agreements; too many unknown factors are involved, including the emotional reactions on both sides.

It is only a *remote* possibility that your letter will result in a particular creditor calling you, in which case you should be prepared for a telephone negotiating session. Try to stick to your original written proposal if possible. Don't let the creditor back you into a corner with a new agreement that does not meet your requirements. Most creditors won't call because it is human nature to accept the payment you have sent along with your plan. You have done all the work, and the overwhelming tendency is for the creditor to accept your proposal because it offers a logical solution for both parties. This is especially true when a supplier has not been paid for a while.

A confirming letter should be sent immediately after a phone agreement or a face-to-face verbal agreement. You should word this letter as follows:

> This letter confirms our telephone conversation of 6/15/92. In this conversation I agreed to pay you $150 each month on the third of each month for twenty-three months, and you agreed to cease further collection of my debt to you of $3,450 as long as the payments are made on time.

From a legal standpoint, a confirming letter is not a written agreement. However, it is very strong evidence of the terms of a verbal agreement. And verbal agreements *are legally enforceable.* The biggest problem with verbal agreements is proving their terms. The confirming letter helps to solve this problem of proof. When you send a confirming letter, the burden is on the other party to write you back and *refute* your letter. If you receive no reply, you have strong proof in court of a verbal agreement.

It is a good idea to keep a log book or journal for a written record of all contacts, copies of letters, dates, and conversations with creditors. This log will be invaluable should you need to prove what was said, especially in any verbal agreements. It would be very unusual if the above steps did not result in some type of agreement. In the rare situation in which your attempts to reach a settlement are not successful, you should get competent legal help in the matter.

How Will Creditors React to Your Letters?

Your creditors will like your offer because they receive a definite reduction of the past-due balance while they continue to get your business on a cash basis, which is a better situation for them than a charge sale, and your letter with your first payment resolves a problem for them: they no longer have to worry about when they are going to be paid. You'll find them more than willing to extend normal credit terms to you once you have completed your repayment plan.

You can count on getting formal replies to each letter you send. In 99 percent of the cases, they will simply acknowledge their acceptance of your plan. Their acknowledgment and acceptance of your plan with a reply letter help reinforce a contractual agreement between you and your creditors. Such a letter is a protection for you should a supplier try to change the terms of your plan at a later date.

Keep all acceptance letters on file. Also keep the envelopes they came in showing the postmarks, and stamp the date received on the letters when they arrive. These items are evidence of the timing of the creditors' acceptance which you may need later for your protection if it becomes necessary for you to go to court.

How to Handle an Irate Creditor

You can resign yourself to the fact that someone will become extremely upset when you approach him or her with a payment plan. This type of person may be the most difficult in a phone call, which may be quite an emotional experience. The primary concern here is that you must not, under any circumstances, yield to the pressure of an angry creditor! Never promise any payment or terms that you cannot fulfill. You must remain calm and stick to your proposal. If you promise anything and then do not keep that promise to the letter, you will be worse off than before. If you have proceeded according to our plan, you will find the typical reaction from your suppliers to be relief. The vast majority of suppliers will work with you and support your efforts.

You Have Now Accomplished a Major Step

Once all your letters are out, you have accomplished a major phase in the process of getting back on your feet financially! You will have effectively eliminated nearly all the immediate pressure and stress from creditor's efforts to collect your past-due bills, giving yourself valuable time and money with which to straighten out your finances. There are few circumstances in which time is of such critical concern as in financial problems. In a business reorganization, indecision and delay can be fatal. You must gather the facts you need and put your plan into action right now.

Checklist Points

1. Be sure you pay all payroll taxes when due. The penalties are substantial and the IRS can simply remove the funds from your bank accounts or seize assets on such short notice that you will usually have no time to react. If you do not have the funds to pay your payroll taxes promptly, immediately make a written offer accompanied by a partial payment.
2. Pay all bank and other loans promptly. You need to maintain good relations with present lenders in case you must make special arrangements with payment terms as a part of your reorganization plan.
3. Pay your rent on time.
4. Make the letters to your creditors a top priority because they will give you immediate relief from the stress of dunning calls and letters. They will also give you time and cash to get your fresh start. But do not offer any terms you cannot live up to.
5. Remember to send the first payment with your letter to re-inforce the contractual nature of your agreement. If you think it will help your negotiations, you may also include additional payments in the form of postdated checks. Just be absolutely certain that you can meet the payments on time.
6. Consider opening backup supplier accounts and establishing a backup bank if you feel it is necessary. Be careful to keep at least three vendors paid perfectly for credit references.

You are now ready to begin a step-by-step, cost-cutting, profit-increasing, stress-reducing reorganization of your business affairs with the primary goals of getting out of debt, getting back on a current basis with all your suppliers, and giving your business and *you* a fresh start!

3

What to Do If You Are Sued

A doctor was vacationing at the seashore with his family. Suddenly, he spotted a fin sticking up in the water and fainted. "Darling, it was just a shark," said his wife when he came to. "You've got to stop imagining that there are lawyers everywhere."
—Jay Trachman, One to One

If you have difficulty with any creditor, or if you find yourself dealing with a collection agency or an attorney, or if you are sued, you may want the advice of an attorney. However, before you contact an attorney, there are steps you can take that will probably resolve the matter without outside legal assistance:

Communicate Immediately

Immediately call the attorney or collection agency and explain that you want to work out a monthly payment plan and send your first payment at once. You will be amazed at how flexible both attorneys and collection agencies can be! I know of one situation in which a $3,500 advertising bill was settled for $1,000, payable $100 per month. The sooner you make an offer *with* a payment, the better terms you will get. The longer you wait, the stiffer the terms are likely to be. But be sure the debt is legitimate, since payment on a questionable debt may be considered an admission by you that the debt is legitimate in a lawsuit.

Make your communication immediate and offer a solution. You'll find most people are motivated to settle with the least expense and legal work necessary. You can avoid most lawsuits if you initiate immediate communication with a sincere effort to resolve the problem. Be aware that any offer you make will be the bottom offer, because in additional negotiations, you will not be able to settle for less than your original offer. Don't be afraid to ask for very small payments or a reduced amount if you feel it is necessary. It doesn't hurt to try. Also be prepared to hint at possible bankruptcy if necessary. This is a potent bargaining tool for your use if a creditor is inflexible, and it is a potential course of action if you absolutely cannot work things out. Most collection agencies and attorneys consider a matter settled if they are able to get some manner of payment. It is the lack of any payments and no communication that usually prompt a lawsuit.

If the debt involves merchandise or equipment, offer to return the items to the creditors. Don't return any damaged goods. If they refuse to take back the items, consider sending the items back anyway. Once they have received the merchandise, you're reasonably sure of getting credit for the goods returned. Most large companies do not have the communication or ability at their receiving docks to refuse your shipment. Just be sure to get signed delivery receipts to document the receipt of the shipment.

To negotiate effectively, you need to understand the bottom-line needs of your creditors. These needs will vary but will usually center on the following points:

1. *The need to reduce losses.* Most creditors anticipate a certain percentage of losses. Your offer states how much they will be paid and when. This is a positive assurance to a creditor and usually stops any contemplated legal action. In your self-reorganization, creditors will have no losses at all but will be paid over an extended period of time.

2. *The need for quick cash flow.* Your plan may not provide speed, but it will give your creditors the assurance of a steady cash flow, which is better than a lingering uncertainty over when they will get paid.

3. *The need for security and assurance that you will pay no matter how long the payment period runs.* Your creditors will typically be more concerned about your assurance that they will be paid than about the speed of your payments. This is why it is extremely important that you *make no agreements that you are unable to keep.*

4. *The need to keep customers.* You are a customer, and your plan gives your creditors an honorable way to keep you as a customer.

Should you decide that you need some legal assistance, you may want to consider a "legal technician" or paralegal, who can help you with routine forms and assist with filing legal paperwork. To locate a paralegal in your area, call the National Association for Independent Paralegals at 800-542-0034.

Going to Court

How to Handle a Legal Summons and Complaint

If all the above efforts fail and you find yourself served with a summons and complaint, don't panic. Starting from the date you receive the papers, you usually have at least twenty days to respond. Read the papers carefully to determine exactly what you are required to do. Be careful not to sign anything agreeing to the claim against you at this point.

You should have the help of an attorney unless the amount of the claim is small and will be handled in a small claims court. Should you decide that you want to represent yourself in a small claims court case, when you go to court bring copies of your letters to the creditor, your payment plan, and any other documentation you have collected in trying to work with the creditor. Be open and honest with the court, explaining that you are experiencing temporary cash flow problems but that you fully intend to repay the debt in full. Explain your plan and be prepared to begin your payments immediately. The court is almost certain to act favorably on your plan (unless it is obviously unreasonable).

Although a *threatened* court action is a bluffing game by your creditor to pressure you into paying on their terms, once you get called to court the bluff is over. That doesn't mean, however, that the claim can't be settled for less than the full amount being sought. An attorney may be able to help you reach a compromise settlement.

How to Handle Judgments

If a creditor gets a judgment against you, the court has given him or her the right to seize any assets or property you may have, or to garnish your wages to satisfy the debt. However, a creditor cannot generally get a judgment against you personally for a business debt if your business is incorporated, *unless* you have personally guaranteed a line of credit or a charge account, or if the judgment names you personally. It is becoming common in many instances for suppliers to ask for personal guarantees from the owner of an incorporated business. A personal guarantee means that you have personally signed a credit or loan agreement stipulating that you are personally responsible for any money owed if your business fails to pay as agreed. However, a creditor can still seize the assets of an incorporated business, which can be just as devastating as the loss of your personal assets.

There are three basic methods used in collecting a judgment:

1. Garnishment of wages or bank accounts.
2. Attachment and sale of assets (sheriff's sale).
3. A keeper, who is a deputy sheriff who stands at your cash register or in your mail room. As cash comes in, he or she grabs it. As checks come through the mail, he or she takes them. The lesson here is never to wait until things reach the state of affairs where you are dealing with such extreme methods.

Garnishments

Under the Federal Consumer Protection Act (which is in force in all fifty states), a creditor may garnish only 25 percent of your *disposable earnings* or the amount by which your *disposable earnings* exceed thirty times the current minimum wage rate. However, you should be aware that this law does not protect a creditor from attaching your funds once you have received them and deposited them in the bank. The law defines disposable earnings as "salary less deductions required by law." Individual state laws differ regarding garnishments, and the federal law usually has precedence over the state law. Most libraries have state statutes that you can check very easily for your own state.

Keep in mind that a creditor, under nearly all circumstances, must take you to court to get a judgment. Exceptions involve signed promissory notes or other loan agreements that give the creditor an automatic judgment upon default. This is called *confession of judgment* and is not much in use currently. In many states its use is no longer legal—all the more reason to communicate fast and avoid letting things get to the court stage.

Who Can Repossess Property?

If you have signed conditional (installment) sales contracts, as in the purchase of a car or specific equipment, you are not the legal owner until the last payment. As a result, a creditor can repossess your car or equipment without going to court. Usually, state laws give you a short period of time to redeem the items by making the past-due payments. If you do not pay at all, the creditor can legally sell your car or equipment to satisfy the debt. However, the creditor must pay you any excess received from the sale after paying the debt, legal fees, and court costs. What is still owed after the sale of collateral is called a *deficiency judgment.*

A security interest is similar to a conditional sales contract and refers to rights or interest in property that are designed to provide collateral to a secured party. As an example, when a bank makes a business loan, it often requires the business owner or representative to sign one or more security agreements that give the bank security interests in all inventory, accounts receivable, machinery and equipment, and "the proceeds therefrom." In effect, this means that the actual assets as well as any money received from the sale of those assets may be legally claimed by the bank. The court's interpretation of how far reaching a security agreement is can be complex. For example, a bank loans money to a farmer and gets a security interest in the chickens (livestock). The problem arises over the eggs—are the eggs "proceeds therefrom?" One court concluded that the eggs were not subject to a security interest.[1] If you are uncertain as to the legal ramifications of any security agreements with your bank or any other person or business, have the agreements looked at by an attorney experienced in business and bankruptcy law.

Most of your suppliers or vendors will fall into the category of unsecured creditors. Unsecured creditors cannot repossess your property without a judgment. Only secured creditors can obtain possession of specific property, which is security for a loan.

Debt Collection: Your Legal Rights and Protections

A debt collector who violates the federal Fair Debt Collection Practices Act is liable for fines and damages. Collection agents cannot harass, threaten, or abuse you. They cannot imply that they are attorneys or that they represent a credit bureau. They cannot call you before 8 A.M. or after 9 P.M. unless they have your permission. They cannot contact other people about your debts and must stop all contact with you except to notify you that they are starting legal action, if you notify them in writing of your wishes to stop all contact except notification of legal action.

Should you encounter someone who violates the laws governing collection agencies, write to the Federal Trade Commission to file a complaint:

Federal Trade Commission
Consumer Protection Bureau
Credit Practices Division
Washington, DC 20580

Wrongful Attachments

Most states require that notice be given before your property can be attached, and that a creditor must first file a complaint stating the basis for an *attachment*. An attachment can include the right to seize property *before* obtaining a judgment, at the time suit is filed. This action is expensive for a creditor and is not used often unless there is a lot at stake, and a debtor might flee the jurisdiction or hide assets. If a creditor fails to obtain a judgment, the attachment is dissolved. You can often end an attachment by posting a bond that guarantees the payment of a judgment if one is obtained.

You can legally recover actual and punitive damages from a creditor who has wrongfully or maliciously attached your property. The reason is that the process of attachment makes it impossible for you to sell your property while it is attached and occurs when there is a *prejudgment* attachment. If excessive property or the wrong property is seized, the creditor is liable for damages to you, but you have to sue the creditor to recover, and suits take time and cost money. Unless the size of the claim enables you to file an action in small claims court, you should avoid this type of action.

A creditor must deliver a summons and complaint to you. If she or he does not, the process is illegal. However, legal delivery now includes the mail in many areas. There are unscrupulous collection agencies and attorneys who never actually deliver the necessary papers, hoping the court will order a default judgment against you for not responding to a summons and complaint. Of course, if the summons and complaint is intentionally never delivered, you cannot respond. In the trade, this is called *sewer service*. The result is you have a judgment against you without ever being notified legally. This is illegal. It can be remedied by a *motion to set aside default*, but you must act quickly! If you ever find that you are a victim of the sewer service business, first go to the court that issued the judgment and explain that you were never served a summons and ask the court to dismiss the judgment, which it may do for you. Today, most judges will still want to hear the merits of the case before it is dismissed.

Legal Limits

The various federal and state laws of personal jurisdiction may prevent creditors from initiating a lawsuit in a geographic area that makes it impossible or inconvenient for you to defend yourself. Many state attorney generals' offices will help you in this regard.

If a creditor repossesses your property, your obligation to the creditor *may or may not* be satisfied despite the value of the property. Laws vary from state to state. In some states, if the creditor sells your property, the law requires the creditor to notify you in advance and to hold the sale in a place and at a time that is reasonable for you. Laws in most states prevent the sale of repossessed property for unfair prices. Usually, appraisal statutes require that the property is appraised before a sale, and the proposed sale must bring not less than a stated minimum percentage of the appraisal value.

Checklist Points

1. Communicate immediately and negotiate some sort of agreement.
2. Offer a solution. Have a specific payment plan figured out before you call.
3. Document telephone agreements with a confirming letter. Keep copies of everything for your files.
4. Have backup legal help lined up just in case.
5. Be prepared to recognize illegal or unscrupulous proceedings.

PART TWO

Reorganizing Your Business

I never got very far until I stopped imagining that I had to do everything myself.

—Frank W. Woolworth

4

Finding a Better Way

Never tell people how to do things. Tell them what to do and they will surprise you with their ingenuity.
—General George S. Patton

Getting a Fresh Start

Now that you have given yourself some much needed breathing space, it's time to tackle each operational aspect of your business. You need to prepare yourself psychologically for this step. Letting go of unnecessary expenditures and other excess baggage can be far more difficult than it seems. Now is the time to think of a new vision for your business, to look into the future and develop a sense of "mission" and clear purpose. Now is the time to make positive changes—to alter the course of events, maybe instituting a completely new company image, or adding new products and getting rid of old product lines, or implementing a new and innovative marketing plan. It is important now to get a sense of direction, a clear concept of the ultimate goals you want to reach over the long run. As long as you're going to reorganize your business, why not take advantage of the situation to really change things, not just fix problems. Think of it as building a new business, the right way.

Let's start with your office. This may seem mundane, but you need a fresh start, too, and staring at the same old piles of stuff isn't going to inspire you with new ideas. Clear off your desk, get a new calendar or desk pad, throw out all unnecessary, redundant records and paperwork (don't stick it in the closet), and put everything away; files, letters, and bills. Vacuum and clean everything, get some flowers, and hang a new picture on the wall; in other words, start with a clean slate. Straightening out your office will do wonders for your frame of mind. You will feel change in the air and in your outlook. Getting your work area organized will help you think clearly and logically.

The first step in decluttering your office is to have a place for everything. Have logically organized files for all records, either filing cabinets or computer files. Keep as many records as is practical in electronic (computer) files. Then, be sure to get rid of duplicate or redundant physical files. Of course, be sure you have a good backup system for all computerized files and records. Get rid of old or out-of-date files and records. Put them in storage if they are needed for tax purposes or must be saved as essential business records.

Next, decide what are the essential and critical items you need on your desk or must have immediate access to. Then, prioritize these items or records so that the most important are at your fingertips. As an example, if all purchase orders must have your final approval, have a priority in-tray for purchase orders on your desk or nearby. Put on your desk only items that are essential to the day-by-day management of your business. During your reorganization, you will want to have immediate access to critical information, which may be provided by the computer. You may want to have your own terminal on or near your desk in order to have instant access to daily reports: sales, receipts, inventory numbers, bank balances, and purchases. Your work area should be arranged to provide you with all critical business information that you need so that you do not waste time looking for important data or reports. A critical element in your reorganization will be knowing immediately the crucial financial data from the daily operation of your business. Without the right flow of information, it will be very difficult to make informed and intelligent decisions. However, don't overload the reporting of information. Just be sure you know the figures that are the key facts.

In a January 11, 1991 article for the *Wall Street Journal,* Peter Drucker wrote, "To start cost cutting, managements usually ask: 'How can we make this operation more efficient?' It is the wrong question. The question should be: 'Would the roof cave in if we stopped doing this work altogether?' And if the answer is 'Probably not,' one eliminates the operation.... It is always amazing how many of the things we do will never be missed.... And nothing is less productive than to make more efficient what should not be done at all."

Managing Time

In a business reorganization, time can be your best friend or your worst enemy. You need to be sure you are in charge of your time, that all time is used wisely and cost-effectively. Do not waste time on nonessentials. Learn to distinguish between what is needed and what is wanted, between what is necessary and what is not necessary. It is often not a question of how many people to lay off, but how to motivate people to work better, to use time more effectively, to be better and more competent at what they do. Wasted time is a devastating expense to a small business firm.

Careful time management means you must first prioritize everything so that the most important tasks are accomplished first. Once you have established the right priorities, you must determine how much time to spend on each task each day. Divide the day into increments and stick to the allotted time for each project. It is amazing what you can accomplish if you spend even fifteen minutes a day on a particular job.

Don't let time push you. You must be in control of time and events. Give yourself some time at the end of each day to reflect on what has been accomplished during the day, and to think about what you need to do tomorrow. Start the next day's work by first giving yourself time to review the work ahead, remembering to prioritize tasks. When you find yourself really overloaded with work, ask yourself, "What is the worst possible scenario if I don't do this right now?"

Organization and Internal Controls

There are three reasons for establishing an organizational structure: (1) to ensure that the owner or management is not overburdened; (2) to establish efficient work flow, with no gaps or duplication; and (3) to prevent internal theft and losses due to disorganized internal control procedures.

Before beginning a comprehensive reorganization, you need to be sure your reorganization is structured in a way that will make your operations most efficient and productive. Salary expense is often the largest expense in any business. Trained and skilled employees are a valuable asset, and you should make the best use possible of each and every talent and source of expertise available to you. Thus a top priority is to make sure each person in your company is in the correct position, where his or her particular abilities can be put to use most effectively.

Delegating Authority

A central issue in the overall success of your reorganization efforts is your ability to delegate authority. You must be able to give other key people the authority needed to assist you in carrying out and monitoring your plan. Without delegating authority, you will quickly find that you do not have enough time in a day to accomplish all that needs to be done. Proper delegation of authority will give you the vital time to work on the most important aspects of your reorganization plan.

Most small businesses don't have any organizational plan. The owner commonly falls into the trap of doing many things that should be delegated to other employees, usually because the owner doesn't take the time to train others in crucial skills or simply doesn't trust others to "do it right." This approach may work when a company is small, but as a business grows, it reaches a point where further growth without delegating authority and decision-making responsibilities to the right persons will cripple the ability of the business to function and may (and often does) result in failure. The owner becomes overburdened, trying to make all the decisions, and, as a result, makes mistakes or simply starts neglecting important areas of operations.

Delegating is essential for business survival. But delegating is worthless if employees are not given *enough* authority to effectively carry out their responsibilities. Your employees must also understand that they are responsible for the use of the authority they have. Routine day-to-day business problems should be handled by your employees, so that you can take care of matters that are suited to your talents and expertise, especially long-term business objectives. If you want your employees to take on greater responsibilities, you need to be sure they receive immediate, positive feedback regarding any situation or problems they encounter. Timely feedback encourages employees to take on greater responsibilities, and lack of feedback leaves employees worried about how and what they are doing, and fearful of taking on any new responsibilities.

A vital part of your plans should be a review of your personnel and their job duties to ensure that you have a proper chain of command with a good flow of communication. Exhibit 4.1 is a sample organization chart that you can use as a guideline for your business. Obviously, individual business needs are different, but there are certain basics that you can use as checkpoints.[1]

The connecting lines are lines of authority. Note that the functions of sales, finance, accounting, and production have independence of authority; the accounting manager is not subordinate to the head of production, and so on. This does not mean that in the company as a unit there should not be cooperation and creative sharing of new ideas or improved operational techniques between the different functions.

Stop now and sketch out your organization, detailing how you have divided the authority, duties, and responsibilities in your business. Then see where you may need to change personnel, jobs, and organizational structure.

Communicating with Employees

If the size of your business warrants it, set up a committee made up of representatives from all levels of your firm. Make your policy one of cooperation and consideration. You will find your employees standing behind the efforts to save your business and their jobs.

Keep your staff informed of the results and progress of your cost-saving efforts. Open communication and honesty will maintain the

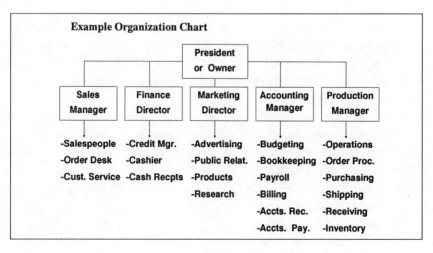

EXHIBIT 4.1

loyal support of those who work for you. There is a natural impulse to keep business problems hidden from employees because of a fear of losing good people and also the embarrassment of finding yourself in a financial predicament. The typical business owner (I did this in my own business) almost always thinks that if she or he waits it out, the problems will go away, especially when there is a recession.

In a recession, the tendency is to wait and do nothing substantial, believing that things will turn around. All the while, the effects of a business slump are accumulating: inventories tend to increase because of declining sales; pricing becomes more competitive, lowering gross profit levels; customers (also coping with the slump) begin to slow down their payments; cash flow begins slowly to deteriorate; expenses climb as a percentage of sales and profits—and suddenly you're in trouble. While all these cumulative events are being absorbed by your business, there is a real resistance to letting your employees in on what is going on. This is a mistake!

There is a serious downside to not communicating with your employees in troubled times: Gossip and speculation begin to prevail. Your employees will sense that something is wrong even if it is not obvious, and they will have your business dead and buried long before you do. Their attitude of hopelessness and concern over something they feel no control over will add further to the downward spiral of your business.

Your employees and key people should be made aware of the problems facing the business before these become insurmountable. Their input and ideas can be invaluable and can help to counteract the effects of a recession or other situations before the problems grow so large as to require drastic remedies. If you do not give adequate information to your employees, they will be unable to take responsibility. Adequate information is a prerequisite for responsible employees.

Keeping your employees well informed makes you trustworthy and credible in their eyes, and this is a real plus in obtaining their loyalty, help, and support. So, do not succumb to secrecy in rough times. You will be much better off sharing the burden of what to do with those around you. After all, their jobs are at stake, and they have every reason to sincerely want to help straighten things out. For these reasons, make your communications frequent, candid, and open with your employees. In any reorganization effort, if your employees do not trust you, you are going to have a very difficult time enlisting their cooperation and help.

Safeguarding Your Property

There are three primary responsibilities:

1. Initiation and approval of transactions
2. Custody of assets
3. Record keeping

A fundamental principle in internal control procedures is that no one person should handle all aspects of a transaction from beginning to end. As an example, a telephone order is received at the order desk. This order will go through a series of steps:

1. *Initiation.* Orders are taken by the sales department or order desk.
2. *Authorization.* The order is checked by the credit department, which makes sure that the order is from an approved customer, that no credit limit has been exceeded, and the customer is current with payments on his or her account.
3. *Execution.* After the order is approved, it is sent to the shipping department to be filled and sent to the customer.
4. *Recording.* The accounting department receives copies of the sales order, the approved invoice, and the shipping documents, using these records to bill the customer.

If possible, different people should handle each of these operations. When you allow one person to do more than one of these jobs, you are opening yourself to potential abuse of your company policies, and the result may be losses and problems. When a different individual handles each phase of transaction processing, it is very difficult for an improper transaction to be completed intentionally.

One simple way to achieve internal control over the accounting functions and the assets in your business is to separate control of these two aspects of your operations. Do not permit the accounting department also to have custody of or responsibility for the assets in your business. The records of one department then become a check on the accuracy of the other department, and there is less chance of disappearing assets or inaccurate accounting records.

In your reorganization efforts, you must have reliable and accurate records and statistics for every aspect of your operations. Without reliable numbers, your efforts will be like shooting in the dark. Exhibit 4.2 gives you a visual illustration of how to separate the responsibility for assets and to check on their reliability. It is not necessary for all three persons (A, B, and C) to be employees. For example, A could be your bank, with custody of cash; B could be one of your employees who maintains records of cash receipts and disbursements; and C could be a computer program that does the bank reconciliations.[2]

Review your internal control procedures to be sure you are not losing money or any other assets through theft, loss of records, or other avenues. Here is a summary of important internal control procedures:

1. Pay invoices only after checked and approved receiving records are complete and attached to each invoice. Be sure you know you are paying only for what you have received! Don't place receiving-department personnel under the authority of the purchasing agent.

2. Use sequential numbering of sales invoices, credits, and purchase orders. This will aid in tracking lost orders and unrecorded sales and will alert you to internal theft of invoices or other documents. If you make a sale and the customer is never billed for the merchandise, you will not be paid in most cases, unless your customer catches the error and tells you about it. Be sure you have a system that will account for all invoices.

3. Do not let the same person count your inventory and also be responsible for the custody of the inventory. Don't let your warehouse manager also be responsible for counting the inventory. As an

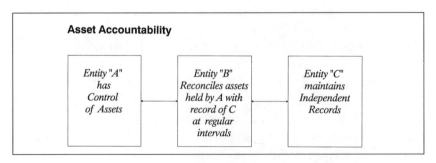

EXHIBIT 4.2

example, a business might have a locked, limited-access stockroom containing expensive, high-ticket items. The person in charge of access to this area should not take part in any inventory counting or record keeping. Disappearing inventory can be prevented by allocating responsibility to different departments. If this is not possible in your business because of lack of personnel, you should have some procedure of spot-checking counts, shipments, and receiving records, either by yourself or by another employee.

4. Have adequate and well-designed forms for all operations: invoices, purchase orders, sales orders, delivery and shipping records, credit memos and forms for returned goods, production orders, and checks. Keep track of where they are and the number sequences in use. This method creates a paper trail and makes it easier to trace errors or theft. Be sure math is correct: extensions, totals, taxes, and freight or delivery charges.

5. Do not let your bookkeeper or accountant also sign checks. Depending on the size of your business, it may be advisable to require two signatures on all checks as a safeguard.

6. Some businesses have invoices with preprinted invoice numbers. If your invoices are prenumbered, you should keep the unused invoices locked up or in a secure place. For instance, access to a restaurant's numbered guest checks should be controlled and monitored. In many restaurants, each wait-staff person must sign in and out for numbered batches of guest checks. Most computer software packages offer you the option of using prenumbered invoices or inserting numbers at the time the invoice is issued.

7. Insist that receipts be attached to all petty cash vouchers. Put one individual in charge of the petty cash fund and another person in charge of balancing or auditing the transactions.

8. Do not allow the sales department or sales manager to have any connection with the credit and collections aspect of your business.

9. Never let the sales department or sales manager have any direct authority over your purchasing operations. If you allow this, you will end up with excess inventory purchased to supply what the sales department thinks is needed for its customers.

10. Void all paid invoices and bills so they cannot be used again.

11. Make it a company policy that all credits and returns be approved by a manager. Do this also for cash register overrings or voids that are over a specified limit.

Checklist Points

1. Set up your office to be an efficient information center—get organized.
2. Establish open channels of communication with your employees. Have regular meetings, memos, letters, or other ways to keep in touch, and make sure this communication flows in both directions.
3. Get written progress reports from your employees or key people on a regular basis. These will give you the current status of your efforts. These progress reports may be simple and informal. In fact, it is better to keep things simple; you will get better cooperation from your people if you do not require complex reporting.
4. In delegating authority, be careful not to violate any of the internal control safeguards. You don't want to set yourself up for additional losses of cash or other assets.
5. Know each day what your priorities are, who is to carry them out, and how and when.
6. Make sure that your internal control safeguards are working properly. Devise spot checks to test the system.

5

Working with Employees

Leaders listen, take advice, lose arguments, follow. . . . I didn't turn the company around. I presided over it. The people in this company turned it around. I was the captain of the ship, but they were doing all the rowing.
—*Irwin Fedries, President and CEO, Monolithic Memories*

Employees Are Your Most Important Resource

Your employees are one of your company's most important resources. They know your business, have a vested interest in wanting it to succeed, and usually have a loyalty to you and want to see you succeed. To be successful, a company must treat its employees with as much care as it does any other critical resource. The first responsibility of all managers is to motivate every employee to contribute to the maximum of his or her potential. A prerequisite to any expense reduction effort is a thorough review of the people who work for you: what they do and how well they do it. If the people who work for you are not highly motivated and properly organized, your reorganization will be considerably more difficult, and it might not succeed at all.

Before you begin this phase of your self-reorganization, invest about one hour in reading a very short little book (about 100 pages) entitled *The One Minute Manager,* by Kenneth Blanchard and Spencer Johnson. It gives you three basic essentials of effective management regardless of the size of your business. Because *The One Minute Manager* gives you techniques that save time and energy, it is especially applicable to a reorganization, where time is so important and effective management is a major factor in a successful reorganization effort.

Many years ago, when I was managing a Woolworth variety store, I developed a simple but very effective management tool, which consisted of a legal pad and a sheet of carbon paper. This particular store was a large, two-floor operation with about forty employees, a large receiving area and stockroom, an office, and a coffee shop.

Each Monday I would start at one end of the store and work my way gradually through the entire store operation by Friday. As I reviewed each employee's area of responsibility, I would make simple notes of what needed to be done or corrected. At the conclusion of our session, I gave the employee a copy of my notes as a guideline to work from. During my next visit, we would review last week's notes and establish a new set of goals. Always I was careful to compliment and express my thanks to each employee for each job completed satisfactorily. Once my visit was complete, I left the employees alone to work out their own way of doing things.

The effect of this method was to educate each employee as to exactly what her or his particular job required. Employees quickly began to anticipate what was expected of them in maintaining their area and in performing their job duties. The immediate effect was that I found my legal pad containing fewer and fewer notes with each visit. My job became tremendously simplified, the employees were happy, and the store looked great!

You will find that this technique, or a similar one, will save you and your employees a lot of time. They will work more effectively and will accomplish more in less time. Using this method, I was able to significantly reduce labor costs as a percentage of sales and at the same time have a better maintained store.

The legal pad method is a highly effective but simple way for you to delegate work and to follow up on the goals and plans you establish to reorganize your business operations. It also gives immediate feedback to your employees, thus overcoming a major defect in employer–employee relationships: a lack of communication and recognition of work well done.

Whatever method you choose to implement and follow up your efforts, be sure you are consistent. For instance, if Friday morning is your day to meet with your shipping personnel, keep the appointment. Make all reorganization management meetings the top priority until your business is completely out of danger.

In setting goals for yourself and for your employees, it is important to establish goals that are realistic. Unattainable goals will quickly discourage and demoralize employees. However, goals should stretch employees' abilities and challenge their ingenuity. This will create a climate of improving morale and confidence and expecting eventual success. As a simplified example, in using my legal pad management system, I had to be careful to give each individual goals that were realistic and possible. Had I loaded anyone with impossible tasks, the system would have immediately broken down, and I would have had a discouraged and angry employee spreading discontent instead of working along with me.

So the guideline in goal setting, both short and long term, is to set goals that are possible but challenging—being careful to follow up progress and give appropriate and *timely* feedback. Timely feedback means that you comment on a job well done at the time it is done, not two weeks later. It is important to be precise and make sure that your employees completely understand the goals; don't assume that someone knows what you want. Put it in writing and get immediate feedback by asking questions such as, "Is this clear to you?" or "Do you have any suggestions or questions about our plans?" Another good questioning technique is to bring out an employee's *feelings* about a particular goal by asking, "How do you feel about this plan?" As an example, if you have just set a goal with your personnel manager to reduce employee work hours by 10 percent, she may be easily able to work out a new schedule, but she may feel terrible about having to do the job. This type of questioning acknowledges your desire to hear employees' suggestions along with how they feel about the job ahead. This simple acknowledgment can work wonders for morale in a difficult time. In addition, immediate feedback at the *onset* of establishing goals may bring to light some unconsidered problem that can then be taken care of on the spot.

Motivating Employees

There are managers who feel that paying attention to negative reactions and customer complaints is all that is necessary. This has a terrible effect on employee morale. There must be a balance between negative and positive feedback. Your employees must know what they are doing wrong and correct it, but it is equally if not more important to reinforce the positive customer feedback and thus, in turn, reinforce the behavior that prompted the positive results. If you want your employees to make an extra effort to please your customers, you need to let your employees know when they receive letters of praise from customers.

A large travel agency in Boston built a "Wall of Fame," a large bulletin board in the reception area that was covered with letters from clients praising the agency employees.[1] The bulletin board gives the employees great incentive to give their very best to each customer. Suddenly employees know that what they do matters, and gets results and satisfied customers who will be back as repeat customers.

Motivating workers through competition with each other results in stress, anxiety, job dissatisfaction, and high turnover. No one likes cutthroat competition. Head-on competition is like a seesaw; when you go up, someone else goes down; one person wins and the other loses. You do not have time for internal competition in a reorganization effort. It will drain energy from productive, cooperative teamwork in which each individual has a vital part to play. In motivating your employees, your goal should be to emphasize cooperation and teamwork—people contributing creatively to make a product or service that is unique and indispensable to your customers. The mark of a good manager is how well she or he can bring out a person's unique talents and help that individual apply those talents in a work environment.

How to Tap Employee Creativity

There are some crucial management attitudes necessary in promoting employee creativity:

1. Managers must encourage constructive, creative, opposing points of view—viewpoints or ideas that may be in direct opposition to the established procedures or the company's operational dogma. And employees have to know that it is safe to express different opinions. In a business crisis, a fresh or different way of looking at a problem is often the key to its solution.

2. Managers need to consider seriously all potential solutions, even when they seem to deviate from the established company policies. Company policies cannot be set in stone and may need extensive changes. In fact, company policies may be part of the problem.

3. Management needs to make time available through the use of planned meetings, suggestion boxes, or brainstorming sessions so

that employees have a concrete way to present their ideas. In these meetings, all who participate should be encouraged to look at problems in unique and different ways. For example, you can look at a problem from the point of view of an employee, from the inside out, or you can look at a problem from the customer's point of view, from the outside in. Make sure all persons who will participate in a problem-solving session know in advance what problems will be discussed so that there is time to think about an issue before the meeting.

4. Peer pressure must never be allowed to influence decisions. A key factor is never to make important decisions by having everyone publicly vote yes or no as a group. Use secret ballots, and have management privately consider ideas and suggestions from employees and then make the necessary decisions.

5. Employees should be encouraged to think about how a solution will affect the entire business, not just one particular area. A particular solution may be great for the shipping dock but may create a new problem for the order department.

6. Tension helps creativity. For example, you can work with tension creativity in your business by having the sales manager sit down with the head of purchasing to come up with a system that encourages sales personnel to do less price cutting and at the same time sell particular items that will help reduce excess inventory. It is a common business practice to separate the sales and purchasing functions of a business because sales people often pressure purchasing agents to buy excess inventory so that they will not run out of stock for their customers. Or simply put individuals with opposing viewpoints together and see what happens. But first establish some ground rules of mutual respect, requiring each side to listen to the opposing viewpoint and to keep an open mind.

An East Coast manufacturer of electronic control systems transformed its business in remarkable ways, increasing quality, profit, and productivity by drawing out the individual, unique creative abilities of its employees. About 90 percent of its 350 employees contribute ideas to management. New ideas earn them chances in monthly, quarterly, and annual drawings for a variety of prizes, such as sports tickets, weekend trips, or a cruise. Their ideas program is a new twist on the venerable suggestion box. The company pays $100 in cash for every usable idea (payments are limited to 10 per person). The employees came up with 500 ideas in 1989, and double the amount in 1990. Ideas that are not usable can enter an awards drawing.[2]

Teams and Groups

Business problems that require fast resolution can often be addressed by short-term employee teams lasting two to three weeks. Each team reports its findings to management. A typical short-term team might be formed to come up with a new type of warehouse shelving that would speed up order processing. This team would need representatives from each part of the business that has anything to do with order processing. Short-term teams are formed to solve problems that are not too complex and that need a quick resolution.

Long-term teams or groups (three- to four-month) are an approach to problem solving to determine the specific cause of a problem. Groups brainstorm different potential causes of problems, often recording them on cards and arranging them in chart form so that a sequence of causal events is visually clarified. When the possible causes are recorded on cards, the cards can be rearranged or discarded as the actual causes are tested and identified. The possible causes are then systematically field-tested, and the results recorded.[3]

The size of a long-term group depends on the specific problem. As an example, a manufacturer of machinery may repeatedly have out-of-stock problems for a particular sub assembly. A group is formed consisting of the purchasing agent, the warehouse manager (inventory control), and a representative from data processing, where inventory and purchasing operations are all automated. After this group comes up with several potential causes of the parts shortages, each possibility is actually tested, the results are noted, and a particular cause is either eliminated or proved to be a contributing factor to the problem. One problem may have several causes. In our example, the automated purchasing system may need adjusting, or the inventory control system may not be accurate, or suppliers may be back-ordering parts. Field testing might involve actually changing the point-of-order quantities, testing more accurate inventory controls, and testing a simplified, faster purchase order system and then seeing how each change affects the problem.

A typical group should be made up of key people from all areas affected by the problem, including different department levels. It helps to get as many different perspectives on a problem as possible. However, keep in mind that in any group, too many people can slow down the problem-solving process. So, persons selected for any group problem-solving process must be carefully selected for particular expertise and talents that will contribute toward solving the problem at hand. Long-term groups work best on more complex problems, where there are likely to be many possible causes.

In their book *Leading the Team Organization,* Dean and Mary Tjosvold explain how to use employee teams to "search for opposing ideas and integrate them to create workable solutions":[4]

1. Include diverse people
2. Establish openness norms
3. Protect rights
4. Assign opposing views
5. Probe
6. Use the golden rule of controversy
7. Consult relevant sources
8. Emphasize common ground
9. Show personal regard
10. Combine ideas

How to Keep Your Best People

The cooperation and best efforts of your employees makes an enormous difference in any reorganization effort. Personnel management and motivation make up an extensive subject that would not be appropriate to examine in depth in this book. However, employee motivation related to compensation is pertinent to your reorganization plans because it involves cash expenditures. You want to economize on payroll expenses while keeping and motivating your best employees. Successful managers understand people and are able to integrate human resources and company objectives so that both the employees and the company benefit from their efforts. In other words, management has to include the human element if it is to be successful.

In a high-tech world, we can easily fall into looking at everything with a kind of cold and calculating computerized view, forgetting that people play the most crucial roles in determining the success or failure of any enterprise. This means that management needs above all to cultivate employee trust through good communications, fair and predictable treatment of all employees, support, respect, and genuineness. Employees need to believe (trust) management. People have an innate need to be understood. One simple way to make another person feel that you are legitimately concerned is to ask "open-ended questions" as opposed to "closed questions." As an example, an open-ended question is, "John, how do you *feel* about the staff reductions in your department?" A closed question calls for a yes or no answer: "John, are you getting the job done with the new staff reduction?" The first question acknowledges John's feelings and gives him the opportunity to explain how he really feels; the second, closed question puts him on the spot: he can only answer "yes" without appearing incompetent. Management needs to be on the lookout for signs of employee dissatisfaction such as poor morale, declining productivity, complaining, mixed verbal messages, and body language.

It is good to keep in mind that money is not the most important factor in an employee's mind. Studies have shown that subjective factors play an important part in keeping morale high. One of these is recognition of a job well done. Robert Townsend, in his book *Up the Organization,* wrote,

> Condition your people to avoid compromise. Teach them to win some battles, lose others gracefully. Work on the people who try to win them all. For the sake of the organization, others must have a fair share of victories. When you give in, give in all the way. And when you win, try to win all the way so the responsibility to make it work rests squarely on you.

I remember one occasion when a good friend of mine who works for IBM excitedly showed me an award he had received at work. He proceeded to unveil a small plaque describing an idea that had improved the design of some computer tape drive. This recognition obviously meant a great deal to him. The point of the story is that money is not the only way to motivate your employees. You may want to consider award plaques for outstanding employees or employee of the month. Often a simple memo or letter to an employee expressing gratitude for her or his work can be a potent motivator. A common complaint among employees is that their work is not appreciated. You could have an appreciation dinner for exceptional employees or mention unusual work or new ideas in a company newsletter. Just walking up to an employee and saying "thanks" can be a big morale booster. A recent study found that performance-based awards are distributed as follows:[5]

- Individuals: 28 percent
- Special recognition: 27 percent
- All employees: 18 percent
- Groups: 12 percent

Compensation

Luby's Cafeterias, Inc., offers a good example of a successful compensation plan that has proved to be very effective and of how to maintain high incentive while keeping compensation tied to actual profits. The company has 160 plus locations, primarily in the Southwest. Luby's also operates with virtually no debt.[6] Each manager has a great deal of autonomy in purchasing and in selection or variation of menu items, depending on customers' local taste. In effect, a branch manager is the head of his or her own independent business. Each manager's income is based totally on profit sharing. A cafeteria's manager gets no salary; instead, he or she receives 20 to 25 percent of the location's operating profit. In 1991, Luby's average manager earned $105,000. Luby's associate managers share in 10 to 12 percent of a location's profits. This management technique has resulted in highly motivated, loyal employees who see a good future with the company. As a result, managers are vitally interested in controlling expenses, food quality, service, and the resulting bottom line, profit.

A zero-salary base would not be practical or possible in all business operations, but it gives you an idea of how such a system can work very profitably for employer and employees. Here is the sound business practice of giving generous compensation through profit sharing and ensuring that management will do all that is possible to maintain and increase profits for the company. A zero-salary base can work well for businesses where individual branch managers are very critical components in a successful operation. A restaurant chain is a good example. This plan would not work well in a situation where profits are either nonexistent or fluctuate by season or because of other factors. As an example, many retailers make most of their profit for the entire year in November and December. There may be a good workable middle ground for your managers in the mix of salary and commissions or bonus pay that will better motivate them to increase profits.

DEFERRED BONUS PLANS. In a reorganization, it is crucial that you keep competent people working for you. A deferred-bonus plan is a good way to accomplish two major goals: (1) to provide incentive and motivation to employees and (2) to conserve cash flow by spreading out bonus payments over an extended period of time.

A performance-based bonus plan tied to specific goals in your business reorganization is an excellent way to ensure a speedy turnaround and also to keep your best people motivated and working creatively. A word of caution is in order regarding performance-based bonus plans: Keep whatever you do fair to all employees. Don't reward chance or uncontrollable circumstances and never "rate" employees.

This cash-conserving compensation approach was described in an article in the *Los Angeles Business Journal*. An employee will think twice before giving up a bonus of this sort:

> In a young business, you basically have two problems. You don't have cash and you need talent. You probably want to use a profit-sharing plan (not a government approved qualified type of plan). A non-qualified profit-sharing plan can equip new businesses with their own golden handcuffs. In a young business, the way to reward people is with cash. That means paying employees extra cash for good performance—but not all at once.
>
> Say an employee makes a basic salary of $25,000. For a job well done, he or she gets a $10,000 bonus—$2,000 paid now and $2,000 a year paid out over the next four years—provided the employee sticks with you. If the employee jumps to the competition, none of the deferred bonus is paid.[7]

EQUITY BONUS PLANS. You can also compensate your key people with equity ownership in your business. There is no cash involved, and the possibility of sharing in the ownership and future profits is a good incentive. Equity ownership is used more often in start-up situations to attract individuals with specific expertise.

Phantom stock is an unusual way to compensate key people in

situations where it is not possible or practical to issue actual shares of stock. You simply draw up a document that (at the date it is issued) has a value equal to the book value of a share or a stipulated number of shares of common stock. The agreement states that as the book value of the company increases, the phantom stock document increases accordingly in value. At an agreed-upon future date or series of dates, the phantom stock is cashed in. You will need legal, accounting, and tax help to set up a phantom stock plan.

Phantom stock has the effect of a deferred bonus and is treated as such by the IRS. It is taxed at the time the employee receives payment. The advantages to your business are a cash saving for the time being and a very good incentive for your key personnel to continue working for the company. If you consider using phantom stock as part of an incentive plan, you should follow these general guidelines:

- Keep the plan simple. Tie the value of the phantom stock to the book value of the business. This plan keeps transactions simple and out of the bookkeeping jungle of trying to compute present values and inflation rates.
- Point out to employees that, unlike normal stock bonus plans, there is no tax bill due until the phantom stock is cashed in.
- You can set up a vesting schedule to help retain key individuals. At set time intervals, a predetermined number of shares of phantom stock is issued. This number can be specifically arranged to suit each individual to give her or him shares gradually at prearranged times.[8]

How to Save on Payroll Expense

Payroll costs can account for 10 to 30 percent of sales volume. As such a major expense, it is a natural and necessary place to look to cut costs. However, it requires careful and thoughtful analysis. Some of your present employees may have expertise that is difficult or impossible to replace. Base your decisions on the Golden Rule. Make it your first priority to keep your employees if possible. When you cut payroll, you are cutting people and altering a person's life. There are many ways to cut a payroll without layoffs.

The CEO of one large company, when he found it necessary to reduce payroll expense, started with his salary first, reducing it to $1 per year. Next, he reduced managerial and executive salaries by 10 percent per year. He did not change secretarial pay rates, but he did work with the union to reduce factory wage rates. Management should set the example when salary reductions begin. If everyone participates equally in cutbacks, employees will cooperate with management in efforts to turn around the business and save their jobs in the process.

Other ways to reduce payroll are to reduce the number of hours worked and possibly to reduce pay rates temporarily. Be sure you let your employees know what is happening and enlist their help and suggestions. Also be sure they understand that the adjustments are temporary. Eliminate overtime pay entirely. You may decide to completely revamp your compensation plan to get the most return from your investment in people.

Autodesk, Inc., a California software maker, realized that by paying hourly rates to many of its employees, it was just "buying time" instead of productivity, the result being lots of overtime pay that was not necessary and excessive errors. The company decided to put its employees on salary with a monthly productivity bonus, which eliminated the incentive to work overtime. Six months after the switch to the salary–bonus plan, errors had almost disappeared.[9] This is an excellent way to switch incentive from just putting in time to concentrating on working more productively.

If layoffs are necessary, give those who are laid off first priority when it comes time to rehire. Consider a plan to help laid-off employees find other work. Try to provide severance pay, or consider letting former employees use your offices to look for new jobs. Have a layoff plan; that is, prioritize the job skills of your employees, and be careful to keep those individuals whose help and knowledge are vital to your business.

Rotating layoffs shares the pain of cutbacks with a bigger segment of your work force. This is an alternative to letting a few employees go. As an example, a Vermont construction company came up with a plan as an alternative to firing ten employees out of a total thirty-person work force. The company decided to ask all workers to work 33 percent fewer hours by taking off one week out of every three. The weeks off are rotated so that the company always has twenty persons at work at any one time. As a result, no one loses a job or benefits, but a substantial payroll saving is accomplished.

In many states the department of employment provides unemployment compensation for persons whose hours have been reduced. It may be possible for your employees to offset some of their reduced hours with unemployment benefits. However, these benefits will probably increase your state unemployment insurance rate and result in higher taxes for your business. You will have to check the regulations in your particular area. In most states, firing or laying off employees will result in higher unemployment insurance payments.

Try expanding job duties so that one employee is trained to do several different tasks. Watch especially for idle time. Maybe the delivery driver can do counter sales when there are no deliveries. In short, do not allow any employee unproductive time. Consider using part-time or temporary help when possible.

If you employ part salary and part commission sales people, consider giving greater commissions and a lower salary. Basing pay more an actual performance and less on a set salary can help both you and your employees. Tie sales commissions to gross profits instead of selling prices. This approach provides incentive to sell at a higher price level and results in more gross profit and additional cash flow and profits.

Use outside contract labor (independent contractors) if practical. You do not have to pay payroll taxes on contract labor. However, be careful to review the IRS rules to determine if someone fits this category. Generally, people are considered contract laborers if they do similar work for other firms, have their own equipment or tools, and are in control of their own hours.

Depending on the nature of your business, you may be able to send part of your office staff or other workers home to work. However, you need to check local state laws. Some state zoning laws restrict the type of work that can be done at home. Modern technology and communications are causing a boom in home-based workers and businesses. If some of your staff can be converted to at-home, independent contractors, you will save a bundle on benefits, payroll taxes, and other employee expenses. You may be able to reduce the size of your offices or production areas.

One successful entrepreneur reports that the benefits of working at home are so appealing that her sixty at-home work staff are even more efficient than her business-based workers. Her company produces guides and manuals for computer systems. Its home-based staff are mostly writers, and she explains how she has made their home-based work force successful:[10]

- Each potential worker's skills are tested for whether he or she has the attributes required for the work.
- Workers are set up in teams (small groups), each with a project manager who oversees the work produced by her or his team.
- Although each worker may work any hours she or he likes, all must check in and keep the central office informed of the hours they have chosen to work. Check-ins are required several times a day, and each person must have multiple means of electronic communication.
- Each person is given highly detailed assignments that show clearly how a job is to be done and what the finished product must look like. Job deadlines are established and rigidly enforced.
- She makes a point of personal meetings with each worker at least four times a year and also has three companywide meetings each year.
- Each home worker is given feedback on how well each job was done.

The use of outside independent sales reps may be a viable alternative rather than an inside sales force that is on a salary, commission, and travel allowance. Recent statistics show that the average cost of a sales call (including travel and entertainment expenses and compensation) are as follows:[11]

- Industrial businesses: $225
- Service businesses: $166
- Consumer businesses: $196

Under IRS rules, an independent contractor must receive a 1099 form instead of a W-2 statement. The independent contractor pays his or her own social security taxes.

Take a hard look at the hours your business is open. Reduce these hours if it is possible to do so without seriously affecting your sales. You might also consider discontinuing a segment of your business. There are mathematical techniques for calculating the effect on profits of eliminating a segment of a retail store's operating hours and also the effect of eliminating what may appear to be an unprofitable division or segment of your business. If you are in doubt, you should consult an accountant or someone knowledgeable about these calculations.

One other way to save on payroll costs is to use an outside payroll service for your payroll checks, tax reporting, and record keeping. These services are so highly automated that it is impossible for a business with even a few employees to take care of all the bookkeeping and tax-reporting requirements on its own without spending considerably more time and money. This is often true even though a business may have a computerized payroll program. A typical service charges $120 to $165 per month for a biweekly payroll with twenty-five employees. See Appendix A for our recommendations.

After making all possible cuts in employee pay and/or hours worked, you must consider savings in employee benefits. Remember, no matter how painful salary and benefit reductions are, they are still better than layoffs. Employee benefits are a significant expense to most companies. U.S. business firms with fewer than 100 employees spend about $1 in benefits for every $2 in wages according to the U.S. Chamber of Commerce. Only 41 percent of business firms having under 11 employees offer health insurance, whereas 82 percent of companies with more than 10 employees offer some type of health insurance.[12] Some of these benefits, such as social security taxes, are substantially unavoidable.

You should look at all employee and other insurance plans, not so much with the idea of eliminating them entirely, but to minimize their expense. This does not preclude the possibility that some employee benefit plans may need to be suspended, if only on a temporary basis, until your company regains its financial health.

Should you eliminate your health insurance? Eliminating health and other insurance is a calculated risk and should be done only as a last resort. You do not want to expose yourself, your family, or your employees to the potential disastrous financial costs incurred by illness or accidents, adding to the existing financial strain on your resources. Health insurance costs are rising at a rate of 25 to 30 percent each year and are a major expense for any business. The average per employee annual cost for health insurance is now about $3,000.[13]

Before selecting a new insurance plan, become familiar with all your options. There are three main categories of health insurance:

1. *Health maintenance organizations (HMOs)*: Under an HMO plan, you do not have a choice of doctors or hospitals but must use the doctor and hospital designated by the HMO. This gives you less flexibility, but HMOs usually offer health care services not commonly provided by other types of insurance, such as nutrition classes and stop-smoking programs. HMOs are less expensive than insured plans primarily because their experience rating system is based on an entire community as opposed to a business group.

2. *Preferred-provider organizations (PPOs)*: These are similar to HMOs but base a fixed monthly premium on the preselected network of hospitals, clinics, doctors, and laboratories, who are under contract with the PPO. Because employees pay some fees, there is less abuse of the system than with other types of health insurance. Patients usually pay a small standard fee for each visit to a clinic or hospital for HMOs and PPOs. These employee fees average $5 for a doctor's visit and $3 to $5 for a prescription drug.[14]

3. *Insured plans, also known as indemnity coverage for fee-for-service insurance*: With an insured plan, you can choose your own physician and hospital. This type of coverage usually comes with a high deductible ($250 to $1,000) and copayments, meaning that the insurance company may pay 80 percent of the bill and you are liable for the remaining 20 percent up to a "stop-loss" ceiling, commonly $10,000. Rates are determined by the insurance carrier's experience with similar businesses and also with your employees.

The easiest way to save on this type of insurance is to increase your deductible amount (the amount the insured person must pay before the insurance begins payments). This will place a ceiling on your potential losses and protect you from a catastrophic loss.

To reduce health insurance costs, make sure you do not have duplicate coverage. Review your business and personal policies for duplications that can be omitted. Before selecting a new health insurance company, be sure to check the financial stability and background. With rising health care expenses, the incidence of fraud is also on the rise.

More and more business trade associations and merchant groups are offering group medical plans designed for the small business. You should check the availability of these plans in your industry for potential savings.

In Ohio, 8,000 small business firms with 145,000 employees and dependents have banded together to form the Council of Smaller Enterprises (COSE) to save on rapidly escalating health insurance costs. By forming such a large group, these business firms are able to negotiate much better prices than individual companies. COSE has now become one of the largest purchasers of group medical insurance in Ohio. Insurance rates for the COSE group members rose only 34.5 percent from 1984 to 1990, whereas group health insurance for the average small business firm in Cleveland increased 154 percent.[15] It would be well worth your time and effort to find out if there is a similar group in your area. The savings in the Cleveland COSE group averages 25 to 40 percent for each business. A well-managed group representing a number of businesses can offer a very good alternative to going it alone in group health insurance.

Another way to cut costs is to use a self-insurance plan. Some business firms self-insure a high deductible amount—say, $5,000—for each employee, and then the insurance company assumes payments. The employer reimburses its employees for deductible amounts. This high deductible saves a substantial amount on premiums. A 100 percent self-insured health plan would be extremely risky and foolish unless vast resources are available. Another type of self-insurance involves hiring a specialized company to handle claims and process paperwork but uses the employer's funds to pay for the medical expenses.

You can have your employees contribute a reasonable amount toward the cost of the insurance you provide. They will have lower cost insurance than they would be able to obtain on their own, and your premium expense will be lowered. Plans where employees contribute a portion of the health insurance costs are becoming more common. An important drawback to a self-insurance plan is the potential of involvement in expensive litigation over contested claims or lawsuits. These legal problems are assumed by a standard insurance company.

Although worker's compensation insurance is mandatory in most states, there are some ways to minimize its expense. You can usually exclude officers or owners from coverage. In addition, worker's compensation insurance is often cheaper when obtained from a private insurance company as opposed to the state fund. The premiums may vary, depending on the current rates, which sometimes make the state fund less expensive. You should check the current rates of a private carrier if you are now insured under your state worker's compensation insurance fund. Check the classification rates being applied to your company. Worker's comp insurance is based on a risk-rating system tied to the job category. As an example, office or clerical workers have a much lower rating than warehouse or delivery workers. It is very common for the ratings to contain errors that cause excessive payments.

If your business can use subcontractors instead of your own employees, you will avoid this type of insurance. You should be careful, however, to verify that any subcontractors have adequate liability insurance. Also be very sure you document each subcontractor's federal identification number or social security number with a signed IRS form W-9 (Request for Taxpayer's Federal ID Number). Recent IRS rules require you to deduct and pay backup withholding if any ID number is missing or incorrect.

Legal Constraints You Need to Know

If your reorganization plans include eliminating unproductive workers, you will need an overview of the legal considerations involved in firing employees:

- You cannot fire an employee on the basis of race, color, religion, sex, national origin, ancestry, physical handicap or medical condition, age, or marital status.
- In some cities it is illegal to fire or discriminate against employees on the basis of their sexual orientation.
- You cannot fire an employee because a creditor has garnished his or her wages. But you can terminate an employee for multiple garnishments. This means that if more than one creditor attempts to garnish an employee's wages, you can discharge that employee. The paperwork that accompanies garnishments is an added burden for any employer and can quickly become a nuisance. Multiple garnishments would indicate serious financial problems that should be explained by the employee involved so that you can determine if the problem is affecting his or her work.
- You cannot fire employees for any action they undertake or

any claim they make under an employee protection law, such as OSHA (Occupational Safety and Health Administration), regulations, the Labor Management Act, or antidiscrimination laws.

- You cannot fire an employee who has been absent from work for jury duty, to appear as a witness (if reasonable notice has been given), or to serve as an election officer.
- Be careful to keep a written, dated record of the reasons for firing or laying off any employee, and place this information in a personnel file. Also keep copies of any notes, memos, and so on that are related to the employee's job duties and performance. These will protect you in the case of future disputes. Keep written records of all complaints and their disposition. These will protect you in case there are later problems. Good records are important in verifying to the unemployment insurance office why a particular employee was fired.
- Mass layoffs have recently resulted in many class-action lawsuits, and recent court cases have tended to favor employees. In a survey by the Rand Corporation in 1988, 66 percent were won by employees. The average award was $650,000. Another California study found that plaintiffs (employees) won 75 to 80 percent of the cases, with settlements averaging $300,000 each.[16] Jurors are making it very clear that shabby treatment during the job elimination process means you are headed for job discrimination legal problems. The point is to consider carefully any mass firings or layoffs because of the potential legal repercussions, which would be an added drain on your resources and time. Consult an attorney knowledgeable in this area before taking such action.
- Deal with employee problems fairly and immediately, before government agencies or lawyers step in. This is the best preventive medicine to avert any lawsuits by employees.
- Set up an employee hot line or an individual as a mediator between employees and management so that everyone has a way to register complaints.

Risk Management

Another way to save money on insurance is to minimize or manage the risk your business faces. Risk management is an evaluation of what areas of a business are vulnerable to losses and how to prevent these potential losses at minimum cost. Commercial business insurance for accidents, liability, fire and other losses can be a major expense, and in some situations, it can become unaffordable or a serious financial burden. The U.S. Chamber of Commerce recently published a booklet entitled "Risk Management," which gives these pointers:

- Consider insurance after all risks and their potential cost to your business are determined.
- Put together a group of professionals to help outline and execute risk management strategies. Include a competent insurance broker to customize insurance coverage. Concentrate on the most significant potential loss areas in the business, and evaluate your insurance needs accordingly, in order of priority.
- Be sure you have done all possible to make your business as safe as possible. And see to it that all employees are properly trained in safety procedures. Make it a company policy to immediately take care of customer complaints regarding possible hazards.
- Eliminate any duplicate coverage. Automobile policies and life insurance policies often include coverage for accidents or death.
- Consider a package policy for all your insurance coverage. A package policy or "business owner's policy" is usually less expensive than separate policies.

Checklist Points

1. Establish teams or groups to work on specific, first-priority problems. Use creative problem-solving techniques. Eliminate competition; emphasize cooperation.
2. Review compensation. Put into effect bonuses, profit sharing, or any other benefits that will aid your recovery without diminishing your cash flow. Consider noncash types of compensation: stock, awards, recognition, or some type of deferred-bonus plan.
3. Review the legal aspects of any potential layoffs or firings. Get expert legal advice before you undertake any significant personnel cutbacks.
4. Look for ways to save money on payroll expenses.

6

Working with Creditors and Suppliers

Our greatest glory is not in never falling, but in rising every time we fall.
—Confucius

Monitoring Purchases

Controlling purchasing is a critical factor in a reorganization. It has a direct and immediate impact on your cash flow and inventory, potentially tying up lots of cash very quickly. If your business has an inventory of products for resale, either as a retailer or wholesale distributor, the easiest way to monitor purchasing is very straightforward: You simply keep a running total of purchases-to-date for the month and calculate this total as a percentage of your sales-to-date for the month. For example, suppose your gross profit margin is 50 percent. On the fifteenth of the month, your sales have reached $100,000. Your purchases are stopped at 50 percent of $100,000, or $50,000, at this point. You can further refine this method by estimating approximate delivery dates. Because most suppliers invoice you for goods when they are shipped, you will have a more accurate estimate of the dollar amount to be billed within a given month. This type of simple monitoring system can be a good first-alert warning that purchases are out of control. In a manufacturing business, inventory control is more complex, but you can still use a similar approach, using actual sales or realistic projections to establish a basic purchasing budget.

Insist on a discount when paying cash for any items. It is not uncommon to get a 5 percent or greater discount in return for cash purchases from suppliers. They are saving the considerable expense of carrying and collecting accounts receivable. Get competitive bids where practical, especially for larger purchases. Try new vendors and compare prices. For this purpose, retain several good credit references. They will come in handy if you want to set up new suppliers or backup suppliers for your business.

Reduce order quantities to a minimum when possible. Your goal is to maximize cash flow, not tie up money in inventory. Order smaller quantities more frequently, and you will put money in the bank. It is often easy to have large orders shipped in small increments and invoiced when they are shipped. You get the volume order discounts but extend payments over several months as the goods are shipped, increasing your turnover, reducing your investment in inventory, and increasing your cash flow.

Many companies are entering into bartering agreements in order to obtain needed goods and services without depleting cash reserves. However, be forewarned that there are many abuses in bartering— a lot of bad deals. So carefully check references and the reputation of any bartering or brokerage company and also any individuals before contracting or agreeing to trade any services or products. Bartering enables businesses to exchange goods or services that they provide for the things they need but do not want to pay cash for (see Appendix A for bartering trade associations). Such trading of goods or services is done at the full markup price. This means that your customary profit is added to your cost so that you have considerable purchasing power while at the same time conserving your cash. As an example, one Chicago bartering company currently has over 1,200 members in its network who pay $500 to open an account that gives them access to anything being offered. In 1990, the company handled $13 million of traded goods and services. The range of products and services obtainable is astounding.[1] One Chicago auto parts company recently traded its reconditioned brake parts for remodeling, printing, and catering services.

Inventory, the Money Eater

When I was at college working toward an accounting degree, one of the professors explained where most small business firms get their inventory figures; with a great swoop over his head, he grabbed a handful of thin air and said, "That's where!" I have found this to be true in many cases, and it is unfortunate that the resulting distortion of vital operating numbers makes it impossible to assess accurately what is happening in a business. Inventory and purchasing are two sides of the same coin. You must first control purchasing if you are ever to get a handle on your inventory. Your inventory should be a profit center. Unfortunately, in many businesses it is a profit eater. This is especially true if your particular business is inventory-intensive, requiring a large inventory to maintain sales.

There is a natural tendency to gradually accumulate more of your slower selling items and fewer of your best sellers. As a result, most business inventories are heaviest in the slowest moving items, the opposite of what you need. In other words, your inventory is out of balance: you have more of the rest and less of the best, when you should have more of the best and less of the rest.

Where possible, reduce the number of items you stock and the quantity you keep on hand to the absolute minimum. As an example, an office supply store often carries thousands of different products, but statistics have shown that only a few hundred items account for over 80 percent of a typical store's total sales. Excess inventory can bankrupt an otherwise successful company.

In a business where sales are rapidly increasing, inventory can get out of control fast. Money literally disappears! In a time of high growth, a business owner easily becomes complacent about the amount of inventory and receivables, thinking that high sales volume will take care of everything. In fact, it is the high sales volume without the accompanying control over inventories and receivables that is the most dangerous set of circumstances in any business operation. Unless you have unlimited funds, inventory management better be a top priority.

A common type of inventory analysis is called an *ABC analysis*. You split your actual inventory into three categories: (1) the items that account for 50 percent of your sales are placed in Category A; (2) items that account for the next 25 percent of your sales are placed in Category B; (3) the next 20 percent are placed in Category C; and (4) the remaining items in Category D.

Next, you determine, by actually counting your inventory, how much you have invested in each category. Invariably, businesses find their greatest investment is tied up in the C category, their slowest moving items, and that the least inventory is in Category A items, their best-selling items. Your inventory ideally should consist of 80 percent Category A and B items. Once you have this information, you have a powerful tool in your hands to reduce your inventory investment. Your turnover will dramatically improve once your inventory is concentrated in A and B items instead of in C and D items, and you will automatically increase your cash flow. Make it a practice to stop all purchasing of Category C and D items. When you sell C or D items, purchase only what you need to fill a particular order. It does not matter at all if you pay more for the item because these categories do not represent the big-sales-volume items and will not affect your overall gross profit percentage.

Obtaining the right inventory balance is a strong motivation to install a good computerized inventory system that will enable you to analyze turnover and dollar investment for each item you sell. If your business is inventory-intensive, I highly recommend that you consider some type of automated system.

Computerizing Your Inventory and Receivables

If your receivables and inventory are not on a computerized system, seriously consider setting one up now, as a part of your reorganization plan. If either your inventory or receivables are out of control, the investment in a computerized system can be insignificant compared to the increased profitability and cash flow resulting from the information and control provided by a good system.

There are excellent computerized invoicing and inventory control programs available. A computerized system will help you to track sales, turnover, and profits and to eliminate slow sellers and excess stock. A good system will continually upgrade inventory records on a product-by-product basis and will enable you to fine-tune your purchasing, keeping the best-selling items in stock and providing better service to your customers while having a lower investment in inventory. A computerized system will give you the critical numbers you need to control your inventory and receivables. You should have a system that gives you the following minimum flow of data:

1. Current inventory level by individual product and total inventory

2. Open purchase orders: merchandise in transit
3. Back orders by product and by customer
4. Turnover by product
5. Customer product usage data
6. Price listing by cost, retail, and contract or sale pricing
7. Inventory item listing: quantity, cost, selling price, and gross profit per item
8. Dollar profit on each sales order as it is entered into the system
9. Item history report: sales by month, year-to-date, and actual profit on each item
10. Low stock reporting
11. Inventory value by product and for total inventory

Higher Turnover Means More Cash Flow

If inventory is a major investment for you, take a hard look at each product you sell. If it sells infrequently or not at all, get rid of it! Until your business is back on sound financial ground, strive for maximum turnover within reason suitable to the needs of your particular business. The higher the turnover of your inventory, the more cash you will have in the bank. Of course, you must maintain enough inventory to fill customer orders.

To calculate your inventory turnover rate (by individual product), divide the total number of units sold in one year by the average number of units in stock at one time. If you are a manufacturer, you should strive for six to eight turns per year per product. A distributor's inventory should turnover at least four times per year. If your business should turn over its inventory four times a year and your actual turnover rate is three times a year, you can return 25 percent of your inventory investment to cash. This can be a significant amount of money.

Other Ways to Minimize Inventory Investment

Have a sale to get rid of excess, obsolete, and damaged inventory items. Offer customers quantity discount prices. These encourage larger purchases, less handling, and fewer delivery stops on your part. You will tend to sell more with less cost and effort.

Consider consignment inventory if applicable to your business. You are not invoiced for consignment items until they are sold. This is getting more difficult to do, but some job-rack wholesalers will put merchandise in a store on consignment, billing the store only when merchandise is sold and the rack is restocked. Some specialty wholesale furniture distributors will provide consignment items or floor samples. Sometimes new companies that are anxious to get their merchandise into retail outlets will offer to furnish goods on consignment to persuade a business to stock their items.

Avoid the temptation to stock up on specials or sale-priced inventory. Buy only when the cost savings outweigh the increased inventory quantities and do not affect your turnover rate. Suppliers are always offering specials for larger purchases, but you can counter with an offer to buy on split invoicing or split shipments of the product, to be billed only as shipped.

Inventory Warning Signs

Analyze the gross profit margins on products or on product groupings in order to spot trends that indicate coming inventory problems. For instance, when a product begins to drop in sales volume, there is a tendency also to drop the price in an attempt to keep moving the product. Conversely, many companies find that what they thought were best-sellers are producing abnormally low profits or no profit at all and consequently find that they must either raise the selling price or drop the item from their inventory altogether.

Watch the turnover on each product. A decrease in the turnover rate is an early warning signal that something is out of control. Poor turnover is an indicator that inventory is increasing in relationship to sales volume. The causes are various: (1) excessive buying; (2) decreasing sales; (3) buying too much of the wrong items; (4) buying certain inventory items that are no longer popular and need to be eliminated and or replaced; and (5) new competition.

It is a simple calculation to get the profit margin on a product. Simply subtract the cost of a product from the selling price and divide this result by the selling price. (A manufacturer must subtract all related costs: raw materials, labor, factory overhead, and warehousing expense from the selling price.) Then divide this result by the selling price to get the profit margin percentage. A manufacturer should be able to generate a 15 to 25 percent profit margin, and a wholesale distributor should make at least a 25 percent profit margin.

Turning Excess Inventory into a Tax Deduction

Excess or obsolete inventory that you have no reasonable way of disposing of can be contributed to a qualified charitable organization. This is permitted under Section 170(e)(3) of the Internal Revenue Code. The IRS requires that the charity have official tax-exempt status as granted under Section 501(c)(3) of the Internal Revenue Code. This is what one North Carolina manufacturer of Christmas decorations does. When the season ends, unsold merchandise that isn't in demand by close-out buyers is donated to local charities. The company deducts the cost of the donated merchandise, plus one half the difference between its original cost and the fair-market retail price. Through its annual donations, the company has claimed thousands of dollars in tax deductions and also reduced the company's warehousing costs.[2]

Feedback Management

Establish with key managers a system for the weekly review of inventory statistics. Your goal should be to create a team effort in the management of your inventory. A crucial aspect of inventory management is feedback from your sales and purchasing departments.

It is vital to be well informed on service aspects: how many orders are filled on time and back-ordered items. Decide the minimum level of order fulfillment that is acceptable for your business, and how long your customers will wait to receive back orders. You may decide you can live with a 95 percent level of orders shipped on time. You must balance both ends: inventory levels and order fulfillment to your customers. If the inventory is too tight, you will lose customers. The flip side of having too much inventory is having too little. With low inventory levels, companies risk not being able to fill customer orders promptly—potentially losing business and worsening their financial situation. Efficient inventory management is finding the middle road, the razor's edge between too much and not enough. Statistics show that most small business firms have more inventory than necessary and that excess inventory tends to keep increasing.

Watch customer complaints regarding shipped orders. Excessive complaints are another warning signal that something is wrong either with your inventory levels or with your order processing and warehousing. Determine your complaint ratio: Divide the number of complaints per month (or week) by the total number of orders shipped. Decide on the maximum tolerable percentage for your particular business. If your business is a service business, divide the number of complaints by the number of billed hours.

Pricing What You Sell

In determining the selling price of a product or service, you must consider all costs that go into the product. The most common ingredients that make up the price of a product before profit are

- Total cost of production
- Cost of service, repairs, and warranties
- Credit terms
- Packaging
- Advertising
- Selling expense

Do not let your sales people set prices. They are inclined to lower prices in order to increase sales volume. Don't buy business and sacrifice normal profits. Anyone can give away merchandise; a merchant sells by adding value above and beyond price alone. Give the best value you are capable of giving in exchange for a fair and reasonable price. Do you need to raise prices? Will your competition allow you to raise prices? Raising your prices will increase your profits only if the new prices do not decrease your sales volume.

Overcoming Price Competition

There is only one way to extricate yourself somewhat from heavy-duty price competition and that is to make what you sell unique. This is called *product differentiation*. In other words, if you are one of ten restaurants in the same general market area and you want to avoid selling on price alone, you must do something that makes your restaurant unique—with atmosphere, decor, or better service. The more you make your product or service different from that of your competition, the more you will be able to add to your price an amount that represents the difference you offer to customers. A product's price in itself may be part of what makes it unique, as in the case of a Rolls Royce automobile, where quality and price add to the product's uniqueness. Quality and craftsmanship can easily make your product unique.

A growing number of companies are stressing a return to quality and craftsmanship that has so long been lacking in many American products. Ben and Jerry's ice cream is an example that is very successful: a high-quality product that is differentiated from the competition. Luby's Cafeterias are unique because of their low prices (creating high unit volume operations) and very fine quality of food. It is quite possible that a lower price with improved quality or some other approach may be the answer.

How the Elasticity Paradox Affects Sales

Depending on the nature of your business, your prices may be highly elastic or nonelastic. Highly elastic prices mean that even a small price change will significantly affect volume and profit margins. Often the solution is to lower prices, increase volume, and generate more profit. Unless you have a semimonopoly on your product or service or sell in a small niche, chances are that your prices are very elastic. If your business has a high percentage of fixed costs that do not change regardless of volume, higher sales volume will give you significantly higher profits. This means that you may be better off with lower prices and the resulting higher volume.

It is an economic law that price and demand move in opposite directions. Thus, elasticity means that raising prices may actually reduce your total revenue and profit because of lower demand. However, if your product or service is low in elasticity, you may be able to raise your prices without adversely affecting your total sales revenue. This is an important decision that only you can make. You may have to do some market research in evaluating competitors' prices to arrive at a correct price level.

Break-Even Analysis

Knowing where your break-even point is makes it easy to project profits and budget for the future. The point where all your costs exactly match your sales is your zero-profit point, commonly called the break-even point. The break-even point is extremely price-sensitive: raising prices will lower your break-even point, and lowering prices will raise your break-even point. Your break-even point will drop as you reduce expenses and will increase if you increase expenses.

To calculate your break-even point, you need to determine two basic types of business expenses: variable and fixed expenses. The fixed-expense category is obvious and includes items that remain the same regardless of sales volume, such as office rent and insurance. Variable costs do what the name implies: they fluctuate as sales go up or down. Examples of variable expenses are certain payroll expenses: as sales increase, more sales personnel are added and salaries increase accordingly. Another variable expense is raw material costs, which increase as sales increase.

There are also semivariable costs that fit in between the other two categories, but we will not go into that degree of detail. A phone bill is an example of a semivariable cost in that it consists of a fixed equipment charge and a variable amount for long-distance calls made.

To calculate your break-even point, simply divide your total fixed expenses by the difference between the selling point per unit and the variable cost per unit. The result is your break-even point expressed in the *number of units* you need to sell. Once you have the number of units needed to break even, multiply this number by the unit selling price to determine the total sales volume needed to break even. For illustration, we will assume the data from a restaurant operation shown in Exhibit 6-1 (a *unit* is the average total sale per customer):

Abel's Restaurant has an average sale per customer of $9 (the unit selling price), total fixed expenses of $65,000, and variable costs of $270,000, or $6 per unit, and it has a break-even point of 21,667 units, or a sales volume of $9 × 21,667 units = $195,003. We can

Abel's Restaurant
Condensed Income Statement

Sales (45,000 units @ $9 each)		$405,000
Costs:		
Variable Costs (45,000 units @ $6)	$270,000	
Total Fixed Costs	65,000	
Total Costs		335,000
Net Income		$70,000

EXHIBIT 6.1

verify this figure by adding the fixed costs of $65,000 to the variable costs ($6 × 21,667 units = $130,002): $65,000 + $130,002 = $195,002, which is equal (plus or minus $1) to the total break-even sales figure of $195,003. This is the equation used to calculate the break-even point:

The formula for the break-even point is

$$\text{Break-Even Point} = \frac{\text{Total Fixed Expenses}}{(\text{United Sales Price} - \text{Unit Variable Costs})}$$

$$= \frac{\$65,000}{(\$9 - \$6)} = \frac{\$65,000}{\$3}$$

$$= 21,667 \text{ Units}$$

$$21,667 \times \$9 = \$195,003$$

When sales fall below $195,000, the restaurant loses money. When sales exceed $195,000, a profit is produced. Also, for each dollar of sales received, 67 cents goes to pay variable expenses, and the remaining 33 cents has to pay fixed expenses and any profits. You can see how a break-even analysis also helps you to determine the correct price levels for the products you sell.

You can use a break-even analysis backward: that is, you can set a desired profit level and then use this information to determine your minimum selling price. This works very well with a spreadsheet because you can just plug in figures and immediately see the consequences of different price levels on profits. The analysis is very easy to do on a spreadsheet such as Lotus 123 or Excel. These spreadsheet programs usually come with sample break-even programs along with graphics in their tutorials. Ask your accountant to make these calculations for you if you are not comfortable doing it yourself.

What to Do with Your Lease

When reorganizing a business, you have four basic options in handling your lease: (1) you can move to a new location at a lower rental rate; (2) renegotiate your present lease; (3) if your lease has not expired, try to sublet all or a portion of the space; or (4) leave the lease arrangement unchanged. Check the terms of your lease carefully for restrictions, and work with your landlord. In Appendix B you'll find a standard assignment-of-lease form for this purpose.

The decision to move to another location must be based on economic reality, considering these factors: (1) total moving costs; (2) how moving will affect sales; (3) what effect moving will have on employees, for example, whether the new location is within commuting range; (4) whether it's possible to terminate the existing lease; (5) what the effects will be on the basic operations of the business (receiving freight, shipments, and deliveries; safety of plant assets and customer access); and (6) whether the move is cost-effective.

A lease is not set in concrete. You would be surprised by how easy it may be to change the terms of a lease. I had the opportunity to help renegotiate a restaurant lease with new terms that were hard to believe. The original lease required a base rental of $4,000 per month or 5 percent of the net sales, whichever was greater. In addition to the rent, common area maintenance charges added another $1,600 per month. The new lease required a $500 rental payment on sales up to $40,000 per month, and $1,000 per month on sales from $40,000 to $55,000. Not until sales reached $55,000 did the original lease terms kick in! In the above situation, the landlord did not want the empty space and preferred to work with the restaurant owner.

Lease renegotiations are influenced by the economic climate. That is to say, if the space you lease is highly desirable and there are people waiting to get space, obviously you will have a more difficult time getting concessions from your landlord, and as a result, you may have to examine other options. However, it is often less expensive and less trouble for a landlord to work with you than to go through the expense involved in finding a new tenant.

The best way to convince your landlord that it is in her or his interest to keep you as a tenant at a lower rent is to have a cash flow statement prepared that realistically shows your present situation before any restructuring efforts on your part. This statement will carry more weight if prepared by your accountant; however this is not absolutely essential. You should be able to prepare your own cash flow statement from your cash disbursement records for the recent month. You can use the cash flow statement you have already prepared following the example of Exhibit 2.1. The Small Business Administration can supply you with excellent cash flow worksheets free of charge (see Appendix A).

In addition, prepare a written proposal stating exactly the new lease terms you would like to have. Be sure this proposal has negotiating room built in. That is, don't make your first proposal your final proposal. It is almost certain your landlord will make a counteroffer. Do some research on current rental rates in your neighborhood. If there are cheaper spaces available, point this out to your landlord.

When you meet with your landlord, bring your cash flow statement, your new lease proposal, and recent financial statements if you feel they will help your case. Be open and honest, but remember it is your job to present facts that will convince your landlord of the impossibility of your continuing in business under the present lease terms. Be prepared to mention the possibility of closing your business or filing bankruptcy if you are unable to work out a new arrangement.

If possible, tie your new proposal to a percentage of your sales. Set this percentage so as to guarantee that you will have a profit before making any substantial rent payments. A percentage rent protects you from large cash outlays in bad months while giving the landlord the chance to profit from your better months. This is accomplished with different percentages for different sales levels, for example, 1 percent on sales of $9,999 or less and 2 percent on sales from $10,000 to $19,999. The best way to protect your profits is to tie the lease payments to graduated sales volumes. The lower your sales, the lower the lease payment. A spreadsheet analysis is very useful because it allows you to plug the different lease rates into your cash flow projections and see what effect different terms will have on your cash flow. Do not enter into an agreement where the percentage rent is added on, that is, a base fixed rent plus a percentage rent. This type of arrangement simply enriches the landlord at your expense. This practice of add-on percentage rents is very common in retailing centers and malls.

Try to get the maximum time possible. If you think you need at least one year to reorganize your affairs, ask for two years of reduced rent. Also, try to get a permanent change in your lease. A permanent change is relatively easy to get, especially if the terms are tied to a percentage of your sales.

You should not need an attorney at this point in your negotiations, but when a tentative agreement is reached, you should have an attorney check the new addendum to your lease before you sign it. Appendix B has a sample addendum you can use. Remember to have all documents notarized or witnessed to ensure that you have a legally binding agreement. And remember, keep copies of *everything* for your records.

Depending on the nature of your business, you can sublet part of your space to another business that may need extra storage space or that wants to share office space. This possibility, of course, depends on the nature of your business. Unless subletting is specifically prohibited in your lease, no consent from your landlord is needed. Check your lease carefully for any wording that limits or restricts occupancy to only your business or to a particular type of business. Sometimes local zoning laws prohibit certain types of business operations in certain areas. Keep in mind that you are still responsible to the landlord for the lease payments. Have the subletting individual or company make its rent payments to you and not to your landlord. It is also important to make sure the business you rent to has adequate insurance.

Keep in mind that in many leases the owner of the store, office, or warehouse you have leased may legally have a lien on whatever you have in the building if you do not make the lease payments. This means your property can be held until payment is made. Read your lease carefully, including all fine print, *before* you start any negotiations or take any action regarding your lease. Do not hesitate to have a lawyer review your lease if you have any questions regarding any part of it.

Negotiating with Your Bank

Generally, you should leave your bank loan as is, if this is possible. It can be dangerous to approach your bank in a time of financial crisis. It may call on your loan and force you into a worse situation or into bankruptcy. It is every loan officer's dread that one of his or her loans will go into default. You may find that your friendly banker is more interested in his or her job and future than in your business problems. If the bank thinks bankruptcy is imminent, it can close your account and remove all funds from your account. This is true when the bank has most or all of your assets as collateral for a loan. Before you approach your bank, I would advise you to set up a second operating account at another bank as a safeguard for your cash and receivables.

If you feel you must renegotiate your bank loan, be sure to present your plan with complete financial information: cash flow projections, operating budgets, and detailed explanations of how you plan to cut expenses and remain a viable business. Make your proposal in writing and in good accounting form. You may need the assistance of an experienced accountant in preparing the necessary information. The burden will be on your shoulders to convince the bank that its money is safe.

Don't try to change the basic ground rules at your bank. In other words, don't expect your bank to accept some collateral that it does not ordinarily accept in its usual course of doing business. If you feel OK about presenting a complete business plan to your bank, go ahead. But if you have any doubts of your ability to present a convincing case, leave the bank out of your reorganization plans. Each bank is very different in its approach to lending. Certain banks specialize in certain industries; others will lend only to companies of a certain minimum size. If your present banking arrangements are not adequate, try to find a new bank more suited to your type and style of business.

I am advising you not to borrow additional funds, but to be sure your present loan or credit line is not in jeopardy as a result of trying to deal with a bank that is not comfortable with your business. You may be able to switch banks and, in the process, obtain more favorable terms (extended time or a lower interest rate) without increasing your indebtedness. This switch will save you money in cash flow.

In looking for a better bank, keep in mind these considerations:

- Does the bank have flexibility regarding lending policies?
- Will the bank give you better rates if you also keep your personal and business accounts with it?
- Is the bank sincerely interested in a long-term relationship with your company?
- Does the bank specialize in small business lending, and does it provide special services for small businesses?
- Would you have easy access to the bank's top management? If not, the bank may be too large for your business. Generally speaking, a small business owner is better off with a smaller bank. It will tend to appreciate your business more than some behemoth institution to whom you are an insignificant and unimportant account.

Understanding your banker's business requirements will enable you to negotiate better. The typical banker looks at your liquidity ratios, debt ratios, turnover ratios, and profitability ratios to determine the financial well-being of your business. The most important liquidity ratio is the relationship of current assets to current liabilities. Divide your current assets by your current liabilities to get this ratio. A ratio of 2.0 (twice as many current assets as liabilities) or better is judged a sign of financial health and is called the *Acid Test*.

Another important liquidity ratio is the ratio of cash, securities, and accounts receivable to current liabilities. This is commonly known as the *Quick Ratio* and is a cash flow measure. You divide the total of receivables and cash by your current liabilities. If the ratio is 1.0, your cash and receivables are sufficient to cover only your current liabilities. A smaller number indicates that you are unable to pay your current liabilities. A number larger than 1.0 means that you have more cash than you need to pay your current liabilities.

In the figuring of debt ratios, the higher the ratio, the worse off you are financially. To calculate debt ratios, divide the first category by the second category. As an example, if your total debt is $300,000 and your total assets are $150,000, the ratio is 2.0, meaning you have twice as many debts as assets. These are the most common debt ratios:

- Total debt to total assets
- Total debt to net worth
- Current debt to total debt (current debt plus long-term debt)

Another category involves turnover ratios. Again, divide the first category by the second category. For turnover ratios, the higher the number, the better your financial health and return on investment. These are the most important turnover ratios:

- Sales to receivables
- Sales to inventory
- Sales to fixed assets

The banker will also look at your profitability ratios. For these ratios, the higher ratio is better, showing greater profitability in relation to sales and net worth. They are:

- Profit (before interest and taxes) to sales
- Profit (after taxes) to net worth

A bank will ultimately base a lending decision on the impression you make on the bank officer. Assuming everything is in order in your loan application, it is your character, integrity, business experience, and the bank's trust or lack of trust in you as a person that will be the deciding factor. Don't add to your bank debt, but ask for more flexible terms. Try to get a temporary period of lower payments, or possibly interest-only payments for six months or a year, or a different type of loan entirely. Keep in mind our long-term goal of getting out of debt.

A fixed-asset loan, also called a *fixed-asset purchase plan,* works something like a cross between a charge account and a long-term loan. One company, The Mike Madrid Company of West Lafayette, Indiana, used this type of financing, not to borrow additional funds, but to make its bank loan more flexible and more suitable to its business operations.

One heavy-equipment company replaced its old loan arrangement with a new $100,000 credit line that was preapproved for specific items of equipment needed in its business: trucks, trailers, and shop and other equipment. The company made a minimum monthly payment on the account of $3,500, but skipped all payments during the period December to March, when business slowed down for the winter.[3] This is an example of how the right bank will work with you and more-or-less tailor a loan to suit the particular needs of your business.

A bank that is lending you money has a strangle hold on your business. The leverage it can exert in your business affairs places it in the position of being a de facto partner. Today, banks are commonly placing limits on a business owner's compensation and often try to control equity ownership of the business. As long as you have any bank debt, you are not in total control of your business affairs.

The paperwork burden for small businesses is increasing as banks are coming under more scrutiny by federal regulators and, in turn, pass on to the business owners all sorts of regulations and reporting requirements. Banks also have access to other information about your business. For instance, they get daily reports telling them how soon the funds you have deposited are used. If you are pressed for cash, the bank is going to be aware that you have cash flow problems.

Your loan agreement may enable your bank to immediately call in your loan if you miss a payment, or if financial trouble jeopardizes your business's credit worthiness. Declaring bankruptcy is usually a defaulting term on most loan agreements. Because the bank usually has most or all of your assets as collateral, it can freeze your account and remove the funds. This is especially true if you declare bankruptcy. The instant a bankruptcy petition is filed, some banks will freeze any funds in the account, even though this type of action is illegal in many states. Banks sometimes ignore these laws, especially in the case of small business firms. And once the account is frozen, you're not likely to see any of that money again. Check carefully the terms of all notes and loan agreements *before* you go near your bank.

The bankruptcy code prohibits a bank (without Bankruptcy Court's approval) from setting off a debtor's deposit account against her or his loan once a petition is filed. The ninety-day rule discourages setoff by a bank if the bank thinks a debtor will file bankruptcy. *Setting off* refers to the practice of freezing deposits equal to the amount of a loan. Because most businesses do not have cash deposits in such large amounts, a setoff usually means that all funds are frozen.

It is important that your bank be stable financially. Many banks are sadly unstable or even insolvent. Ask for regular financial statements from your bank, and make sure its finances are sound. It is advisable to maintain two banking connections as a safeguard in case of problems. Maintaining a payroll account at a different bank is an easy way to keep another active account, and it is a good internal control practice to separate your payroll account from your regular operating account.

In 1990 1,069 banks were on the government's problem list with assets of $611 billion; that is, they were essentially insolvent and at risk of closing and did not have enough assets to cover deposits.[4] For $29 you can order a listing of safe banks from Command Productions, P.O. Box 2223, San Francisco, California 94126 (phone: 415-332-3161). Check Appendix A for other agencies that furnish information on the financial standing of banks in specific areas. When checking on a particular bank:

- Watch out for banks that offer above-average (above current market rates) premiums or interests for deposits. This offer may be a sign that the bank is making risky loans. Remind yourself that higher returns equal higher risks.
- Be on the lookout for management or operational changes at your bank. These may be a signal that banking regulators are forcing changes and are a definite danger sign.

- Make sure your bank is federally insured. If it is federally insured, the law requires it to post in a public area the FDIC or FSLIC signs.
- Do not keep over $100,000 at one bank without making sure that any excess over $100,000 is also insured. Ask to see evidence of such insurance in writing.

Factoring as an Alternative

Because of the strings attached to any bank loan, many business owners look for other sources of cash. Factoring may be a viable alternative to bank financing, especially if you have been turned down for a bank loan. In a factoring arrangement, you sell (assign) your accounts receivable to a factor or third party, which then collects the funds from your customers. You are paid immediately for your receivables as you generate invoices for your product or services. The factor makes its profits by discounting your receivables; that is, the factor buys your receivables at a discounted price.

The factoring company that buys your receivables is interested only in how credit-worthy your customers are, not in your ability to repay a loan. In fact, factoring is not really a loan; it is a simple purchase of the receivables you have generated. However, you may have difficulty factoring your receivables if the bank already has your receivables as collateral. Thus you may need first to pay off the bank loan before you can enter into a factoring agreement.

The discount rate is the set percentage of your receivables that the factor keeps as its fee for advancing you the funds. If you can afford the discount rate, this arrangement can be a fast source of cash. As an example, one large factoring company charges a 2 percent discount rate for each 15-day time period that elapses in the collection process. If a bill is paid within 15 days, the fee (per month) is 2 percent; within 15 to 30 days, 4 percent; and within 30 to 45 days, 6 percent. The catch in factoring is that the cost will be much more than that of a bank loan. The factoring company must account for slow and uncollectible receivables in its discount rate. Factoring can take the pressure off financing rapid sales growth with the resultant mushrooming receivables. Selling your accounts receivable basically eliminates the normal 45-day period it takes to convert inventory into cash. Factoring is not meant to be a long-term solution to cash shortages, but it may be a short-term alternative while a business reorganization is in process. It may provide some necessary breathing space. The advance rate is the amount of up-front cash the factor will advance you immediately for your receivables. This rate varies according to the credit standing of your customers. The highest rate you can expect is 80 percent if the quality of your receivables is excellent, with very few bad debts.

There are two basic types of factoring: *with recourse* and *without recourse*. The first method means that the factor can come back to you as a final recourse in collecting the accounts; in other words, you are still responsible. If an account does not pay, you must buy back the account for the balance still owed. The without-recourse method means that the factor has no recourse to you if someone does not pay. This is the best method, but of course it is usually the more expensive way.

If you have pledged your accounts receivable as collateral for any loans, you cannot assign them to another party without the consent of the lender and the agreement of the factoring party to the lien on the receivables. You should consider factoring only as a last resort. The discount rate you are charged may be two or three times the prime bank lending rate. You have to be able to absorb this additional cost in your profit margin.

You can also damage the relationship you have with your customers by allowing a third party to become involved in the process of collecting your accounts receivable. This is especially true if your business is built on your personal contact with customers. Most factors have stringent collection procedures, and they will not hesitate to call your customers about past-due bills.

Factoring your receivables can hurt your reputation. Many people assume you are in some sort of financial difficulty when any third party takes over the responsibility of collecting your receivables. This assumption may damage your sales at a time when you can least afford it. If your customers begin to doubt your ability to remain in business, you may suffer a fatal drop in sales.

There are a number of ways to infuse cash into your business without any more borrowing. You can look for investors. You may have friends or relatives who would be interested in investing in your business. If your business troubles stem from a lack of operating capital due to rapid growth, an outside investor may be an excellent choice, especially one who also has experience in your particular industry. Some states are passing legislation that allows small firms to sell stock to the public.

Venture Capitalists

If circumstances are such that a venture capitalist firm might be interested in your company, you should be aware of the concessions a typical firm will demand. It will expect equity ownership in your company, plus preferred stock, voting control, and other special rights. In other words, you may get the money you need, but in the exchange, you will lose control of your business.

There is an informal network of investors (sometimes called *angels*) who supply new and growing businesses with three to four times the amount of funds that venture capital companies usually put up. These investors are usually wealthy individuals who have made their own money in the business world. Most investors of this type are in their sixties and rarely under forty. They often own their own business and look for investments in similar businesses or areas that they are familiar with. A recent survey found that there are approximately 1 million millionaires and that about 250,000 of these millionaires invest in new and growing businesses. The same survey found that there are about 400,000 informal investors who invest 10 to 20 percent of their net worth in this way. About 20 percent of these individuals invest cash ($10,000 to $100,000 per business), and about 80 percent also participate in the management of the company, either as a board member or sometimes as an employee.[5] Many of these informal investors work as advisers to a business, and because they usually have lots of practical experience behind them, they can be a valuable asset for a business.

So, how do you find your angel? You must start asking people you know: friends and business acquaintances. And ask these people to ask people they know to ask also. Ask accountants, attorneys, or financial advisers—anyone who may have clients who are looking for investments. Check with leading business figures in a similar type of business. Ask your banker only as a last resort, unless your rapport with your bank is such that you can approach it easily on the subject without jeopardizing your banking arrangements. The two primary advantages of an informal investor are (1) they usually do not ask for as large a chunk of a business as do the professional venture capitalists, and (2) they will often provide valuable management and business expertise.

Checklist Points

1. Get creditors off your back right away. You will not be able to spend the time needed in a reorganization if you're on the phone all the time fending off collection efforts.
2. Gain control of purchases, inventory, and receivables immediately.
3. Review your pricing very carefully, along with your break-even point. Are your prices too high or too low, or just right?
4. Look at alternate sources of cash: subleasing, equity investors, venture capital, partners, factoring, or the possible sale of certain unnecessary assets.

Working with Customers

Doing business without advertising is like winking at a girl in the dark.
You know what you are doing, but nobody else does.
—*Steuart Britt,* New York Herald Tribune, *October 30, 1956*

Managing Your Accounts Receivable

Your cash flow is easily decimated if you do not collect money owed you within the terms of sale established by your business. Financing accounts receivable and inventory is a major drain on cash flow.

Accounts Receivable Guidelines

- Put slow payers on COD until their account is current.
- Always check credit before shipping orders.
- Establish credit limits for all slow payers.
- Require partial or full prepayment on all new accounts.
- Get cash deposits from new customers and on special orders if possible.

Sales that are not cash sales consume cash through the resulting replenishment of inventory and the usual payment of your purchases before receiving payment from your customer. This is why so many successful companies fail in the midst of skyrocketing sales. Often the only way to save a business from a disastrous capital shortage is to put a brake on sales increases until the necessary capital accumulates or is obtained through some sort of capital infusion.

If your business is inventory-intensive, every charge account is forcing you to expend money in one form or another. This is why control of receivables and careful monitoring of inventory are critical ingredients in all successful businesses.

Aging Receivables

Slow-paying charge customers can drain your cash in short order! You should be tactful but firm in requiring your customers to pay on time. You're not in the loan business. Make sure your accounts receivable are under control. If your receivables are older than forty-five days on the average, you need to work on speeding up payments. To calculate the average age of your accounts receivable, divide your total accounts receivable amount by your average monthly sales volume; then multiply the result by thirty days. Here is an example:

> Total accounts receivable: $150,000
> Divided by average monthly sales of $62,500 = 2.4
> Multiply 2.4 by 30 days to get 72 days as the average collection time.

If your business, like most, has to pay its bills within thirty days, you cannot afford to allow your customers seventy-two days to pay their bills. The money you need to pay your bills on time has to come from somewhere. This is precisely the reason that receivables are a vital area of concern and require constant attention in any reorganization effort. Find out who is borrowing lots of interest-free money from you.

A necessary element in controlling your receivables is to prepare an accounts receivable aging report. This report will list each customer, its current balance owed, and how much past due the account is. This can be done manually from customer ledger cards but is most easily done with a computerized system. Exhibit 7.1 is an example of a typical aging report.

You or whoever is in charge of your credit department should have a set procedure for reviewing all past-due accounts, making calls, sending past-due notices, and following up on promised payments. This should be done weekly, or more frequently if needed. Once you have accurate and timely receivables figures, you can eliminate chronic late-payers, and you can also flag accounts whose monthly volume does not warrant carrying them on a charge basis.

					Widgets, Inc.				
					Accounts Receivable Aging Report				
					4-30-92				
Invoice No	Inv Date	Amount	Payments	Credits	Balance	1-30	31-60	61-90	90 +
** ABCDAT * ABC DATA, INC. * (303)787-1720									
10767	03/09/92	1107.00	0.00	0.00	1107.00	0.00	1107.00	0.00	0.00
10777	04/06/92	37.57	0.00	0.00	37.57	37.57	0.00	0.00	0.00
** Subtotal**		1144.57	0.00	0.00	1144.57	37.57	1107.00	0.00	0.00
** XLSYST * XL SYSTEMS * (303)555-8891									
10655	02/10/92	122.75	0.00	0.00	122.75	0.00	0.00	122.75	0.00
** Subtotal **		122.75	0.00	0.00	122.75	0.00	0.00	122.75	0.00
*** Total ***		1267.32	0.00	0.00	1267.32	37.57	1107.00	122.75	0.00

EXHIBIT 7.1

Your receivables are potentially a big source of fresh cash when properly managed. Normally a good accounts receivable aging report includes individual invoice numbers so you can isolate unpaid bills at a glance.

Speeding Up Collections

Give your customers some incentives for paying you faster. Offer them a 2 percent discount if their bill is paid within ten days; offer a larger discount for cash. You can also offer a cash discount as an alternative to accepting credit cards. For example, if your merchant fee for a particular card is 4.5 percent, offer your customer a 2 or 3 percent discount for cash.

Get sufficient deposits from customers for special orders. These immediately provide you with more operating cash. As an example, an office furniture store can easily get a 50 percent up-front deposit for most orders. A printer can easily get a 50 to 100 percent deposit for printing orders, especially when the customer is new or the order involves expensive or special materials. But remember that you may have to refund all deposits if you close your business.

Speed up your order processing. Collecting your receivables quickly has a dramatic effect on your cash flow. You need to do everything possible to reduce the gap between the time merchandise is purchased and the time it is sold. One way to do this is to process each order as fast as possible while maintaining accuracy and quality. Do not wait to invoice a customer because one item is back-ordered. Instead, bill your customer for the items shipped, and when the back-ordered item arrives, generate a separate invoice for the back-ordered item or items.

Collecting Past-Due Accounts

Remember that a good collection system is a process, not just one letter without prior communication. You should have a planned series of steps: a friendly reminder, past-due statements, phone calls, and, as a last resort, a final letter like the example in Exhibit 7.2. It is better to accept a series of payments on a past-due account from a customer who is experiencing temporary difficulty and keep him or her as a good customer than to cut the customer off without any attempt to work out an agreement. It is the chronic, unresponsive, noncommunicative, nonpaying customer who must be weeded out of your receivables. Does it pay to do your own bill collecting? Absolutely! Statistics show that you can expect to average about 12 cents back on each dollar you turn over to a collection agent.

Establish a definite system to follow up on past-due accounts. A letter is always much better than a rubber stamp or a sticker. A personal telephone call from you to the person responsible for payment is the best way to approach the matter. If possible talk to the owner or manager and be firm but polite. Remember always to treat another business with the same courtesy you would like to receive. If this still does not work, you will have to stop selling to this customer on a charge basis.

It is true that many companies will pay only those suppliers who diligently follow up on late payments and will let go, for as long as possible, payments to suppliers who never complain or send any notices—all the more reason for you to set up a definite process with proper follow-up.

There is an effective way to get payment from even the most difficult accounts. After you have sent a friendly reminder and another past-due notice, send a letter (see Exhibit 7.2) to the account with the clear message: "If payment is not received within a stipulated period (ten days or less), you will be forced to turn the matter over

Able Supply Company
1200 Profit Ave.
Yourtown, CO 80210
(303)341-3055 FAX (303)341-9956

4/22/92

Attn: Mel Nasrudin
Avoidance Industries
644 Pit Road
Los Vegas, Nevada 84020

Re: Past Due Balance: $3,850.75

Dear Mr. Nasrudin:

We have not received payment on your account, which is now seriously past due. Our not having heard from you regarding payment arrangements in spite of our numerous calls, is not acceptable. In a few days we will have no choice other than to proceed with the necessary legal steps. Your business has been important to us. As you might imagine, this choice is one that we do not take lightly however, I think you will agree our position is a fair one. We have been happy to extend credit to your firm based on your promise to pay according to our terms. We trust that you will give this matter your immediate attention.

Our company is reluctant to take any action that might jeopardize your reputation and credit record and cause you embarrassment or additional expense. As you know, our contract stipulates that you are responsible for all collection and legal fees.

I am counting on your prompt action and receiving your payment IN FULL IMMEDIATELY. Payment (in cash or certified funds) must be received in our office by 5:00 P.M. on or before May 2, 1992, in order to stop automatic legal proceedings from being initiated against Avoidance Industries and you personally as president and owner.

Very truly yours,

Henry Hardman,
Credit Manager
Able Supply Company

Copy: Lavroth and Crusher, Attorneys at Law

EXHIBIT 7.2

to your attorney." It is also a good idea to be exact about your time limit: "by May 23, at 5:00 P.M." You should set a maximum past-due number of days for your receivables. In most cases (there are industry variants), you should not allow any account to exceed sixty days past due. If your normal terms are thirty days, then at the thirty-five-day point your collection system should begin.

At the end of the letter place this phrase: "Copy: Lavroth & Crusher, Attorneys at Law." This notice at the bottom of the letter warns your customer that legal action has possibly already begun. You do not need actually to send a copy of the letter to your attorneys. Just let your attorneys know you may be notifying some of your customers of pending legal action and will be keeping them informed as the need arises.

Address this letter to the owner or CEO. Do not send it to a department or address it: "Attn: Accounts Payable." Direct it to the responsible individual. Also, never use the phrase, "Please ignore this request if your check has already been mailed," which just guarantees quick filing in the nearest trash bin.

It is important to send this letter by certified mail, with a return receipt requested. This shows your customer that you are serious, and it also makes the letter a legal notification should eventual legal action be required.

The example letter (Exhibit 7.2) should be modified to suit your particular requirements, but the essential flavor of the letter should be maintained. This style of letter should be sent only after normal attempts to collect on an account have failed. Once you send a letter of this sort, be very careful to follow through on your terms. You must be prepared actually to give the account to your attorney or a collection agency. The worst thing you can do is to not enforce the terms of your letter.

Controlling Receivables

All your cost-cutting efforts will be useless if your receivables are not tightly controlled. You will be like the man trying to get water from the well with a hole in the bucket! At this point in your reorganization plan, you are better off without slow or nonpaying accounts. Of course, you must have adequate controls before you open a charge account for another company or individual. Be sure you check credit references and payment history carefully. The credit form should clearly stipulate your payment terms. This is especially helpful in case you need to use legal means to collect an account. In small claims court the winner will be the one with the best documentation of the facts.

You may want to consider subscribing to one of the commercial credit-rating services available (such as Dun & Bradstreet). They provide credit and financial information on most U.S. business firms. Their fees vary depending on the services provided, but they may save you a lot of money in the long run, especially if your business has high individual billings or a large investment in total accounts receivable. Fees for commercial credit-rating services average $14 and up per report; credit reports for individuals average $15 to $20 per report.

It is important to have a written credit application that each new account must complete (see Exhibit 7.3). After a new charge customer has signed your application for credit, keep the original and give a copy to the applicant. It is inevitable that you will run into a business owner who is insulted by the request to fill out your application. For this reason it is better to have someone other than yourself or a sales person handle the application procedure. This person should simply state that this is a set company policy and that all new accounts must fill out an application. It is essential that the customer not feel resentful of the sales person or the owner of the business.

It is much better to have one of the office staff handle all credit and collection work, as opposed to an owner or a sales person who is more directly involved with customers. For example, a sales person will usually find it difficult to enforce payment terms out of fear of losing the account. Office personnel will be much more detached in their collection efforts, and the customer will usually not direct any anger at the sales person.

To safeguard your investment in addition to the cost of running a credit check, it is not at all uncommon to request that a new customer's initial order be cash in advance while their application is being processed. Most new accounts will understand this request, especially if the company is new, is not well known, or has a similar policy with its own new accounts. Of course, once you have approved the account, be sure to send a welcoming letter to the new customer, thanking her or him for opening the account.

Marketing: What Is It?

Marketing is not advertising, although the marketing process includes advertising and promotion. Marketing educator and founder of the department of marketing at Bowling Green State University, Maurice Mandell defines marketing as: "An exchange process between producers and consumers, in which the producer matches a market offering (the product or service, plus its price, distribution, and

Application for Credit and Agreement to

Please complete and return to:
1200 Profit Ave., Yourtown, CO 80210
(303)241-3034   FAX(303)242-8099

ABLE SUPPLY
COMPANY

Legal Business Name:				
Address:	City:		State:	Zip:
Phone:	Fed Tax ID No:		State Tax No:	
Type of Business:				
Number of years in business:		How long at this address:		

PARTNERSHIP OR PROPRIETORSHIP:

Name:	Social Sec #	Home Address
1.		
2.		
3.		

CORPORATION:

Title:	Social Sec #	Home Address
President:		
Vice President:		
Secretary:		
Treasurer:		

PRINCIPAL SUPPLIERS:

	Phone No.	Address
1.		
2.		
3.		

BANK:	Phone:	Officer:
Address:		

AGREEMENT:

If credit is granted, we promise to pay all bills within 30 days of the invoice date as stipulated by Able Supply Co. In the event payment is not made and this account is referred to a collector for collection, we agree to pay all costs of collection. Applicant also understands that interest on any unpaid balance will be charged at the highest rate authorized by law. If suit or action by an attorney is instituted, we promise to pay all attorney fees in said suit or action.

The undersigned jointly and severally personally guarantee the payment of all amounts set forth above:

Owner/Corporate Officer/Co-Partner

Authorized Agent for
Able Supply Company

Personal Guarantor

EXHIBIT 7–3

promotion) to the wants and needs of the consumer."[1] This concept does not refer just to a product line but also refers to identity, mission, and direction. Where is your business going and what are its long-range goals? A good marketing strategy will play an important part in helping your company to realize its full potential in all these areas.

The basic marketing functions are

1. Assembly, transportation, and product distribution
2. Storage and financing
3. Promotion, selling, and advertising
4. Customer contact and finalization of sale
5. Price and terms of sale

All these basic marketing functions directly or indirectly affect operating expenses. Each aspect of your marketing functions should be reviewed for whether any expense can be reduced or eliminated.

Marketing Essentials: A Self-Quiz

1. Are your products or services correctly matched to the customer who needs them? You may need to conduct a market survey to determine whom you should reach with your advertising and where your customers are located. If you don't know what your customers want, you have to find out.

2. Are your services or products assembled, transported, and delivered in the most cost-effective manner possible while you maintain the best quality, service, and craftsmanship?

3. Is your advertising cost-effective? Is it an expense or a profit producer? Does your advertising educate customers about your products or services? Is it direct and honest?

4. How are customers treated, and how are sales finalized? How do you handle complaints and returns?

5. Are your prices competitive? Are your selling terms competitive? Do you know your competition's prices and terms? Do your prices properly reflect the quality and service offered?

6. Are your sales terms and financing reasonable, and are they conducive to completing a sale?

7. What business are you in? Believe it or not, many business owners would have difficulty answering this question. It is a fundamental marketing principle that you must define exactly what your business is before you can attempt to market your products or services effectively. Often, a business enterprise loses its original purpose, becoming scattered or so diversified that it becomes difficult to describe accurately exactly what the business is doing.

8. Do you take care of customers after the sale? Do you provide adequate service and warranty for your products? Customer support after a sale can mean the difference between success and failure in any business.

Keeping Your Customers

The cost of obtaining a new customer is a major expense to most businesses and must be reflected in your cost-cutting efforts. Unless your business is producing and keeping satisfied customers, you have an added expense burden of constantly trying to replace customers.

Jack Weissman, a sales and customer service consultant in East Northport, New York, explains, "Sales starts a customer relationship. Service turns it into a profitable or unprofitable relationship. With the high cost of obtaining a new account these days, unless it's long-standing, it's usually an unprofitable relationship. You can set up your customer service as a profit center. You know what it costs to acquire a customer—you can track it with your sales team. Any time you retain a customer, you've reduced your overall acquisition costs."[2]

Research shows that about 70 percent of the business of most business firms is from repeat customers.[3] This means that the majority of your customers come to you because they have a positive memory of their last visit to or transaction with your company. Remember that the average customer will not call to complain about a product or service: she or he simply never returns.

Ultimately it is people who make or break a good customer support program. Alan Offner, a management consultant, says, "The main thrust of customer service isn't the nitty-gritty things. The basic attitudes of the employees are more important." It is imperative that you have competent, patient, and sincerely concerned people handling your customer support services. In a world of increasing technology with computerized answering systems, human contact becomes more sensitive and more important. Everyone wants to be treated with respect and feel that her or his business is appreciated. Each customer's problem must be viewed as a top-priority item to be resolved quickly and efficiently.

Product Guarantees

The very successful catalog company L. L. Bean has centered its way of doing business on its company credo: "Sell good products at a reasonable profit, treat your customers like human beings, and they will always come back." L. L. Bean's customers rely on Bean's money-back product guarantee: they can return any item at any time and for any reason. A spokesman for L. L. Bean said, "We would rather have a customer return something than throw it in a closet and never buy anything from us again."[4]

Finding Out What Your Customers Need: "Dialogue Marketing"

The more you zero in on the needs of your customers, the easier it will become to keep customers and increase repeat business. The more repeat business you develop, the lower your selling expenses will be. And that is what we are aiming at: lowering all aspects of business expense as a percentage of sales volume.

It is essential to establish a dialogue with your customers so that you are at all times aware of their needs and are also alerted to potential problems before they become disasters. Customer feedback may be initiated by phone, by questionnaires, or by a simple reply card stuffed in a customer's order that says, "Let us know how we are doing."

Domino's Pizza sends thank-you post cards to its customers asking for comments on its food and service. Bonnie MacEachern, a customer service agent for Arrow Messenger Service in Chicago, spends a lot of her time calling Arrow's customers, asking "How are we doing?" She adds, "It has proved to be the most effective way for us to find out what our customers want, and that's our job."[5] You must have feedback on how well your business is satisfying customers. You need to find an economical way to sample customers on a regular basis. It is also important to check all complaints to determine the causes and to take needed corrective measures.

Customers of Federal Express are polled daily and asked to rate important aspects of customer service. A Federal Express spokesman, Armand Schneider, said, "Our goal is to achieve 100 percent customer satisfaction."[6]

Advertising Purpose and Fundamentals

The basic function of advertising is to inform potential customers of the products or services you offer and to distinguish them from those of the competition. If no one knows your business exists, it will not be around long. In a business reorganization, the decision to cut advertising expense may be a big mistake. The major goal is to make your advertising pay for itself and generate new business. You must carefully scrutinize your advertising to eliminate unnecessary and unproductive ads. In a reorganization, every ad dollar must work overtime for you.

Follow the Five Advertising Fundamentals

In each ad there is a hierarchy of effects that persuades someone to buy your product. One of the most common principles is known as *AIDA,* which is an acronym representing the sequence of steps that effective ads follow. Be sure your advertising follows these advertising fundamentals:

A —Get *attention.*
I —Create *interest.*
D —Stimulate *desire.*
A —Ask for some type of *action.*

Another version of the AIDA formula extends it somewhat in this five-step formula:

1. Get attention.
2. Show people an advantage(s).
3. Prove it.
4. Persuade people about the importance of the advantage(s).
5. Ask for some type of action.

Your ad must first get attention and be read or heard if it is to be successful. It must stand out from the crowd. In other words, if you don't get people's attention, the best ad in the world will be wasted money. Advertising, especially for a business in trouble, must be cost-effective. You cannot afford to generalize about your products or image. You need to be specific; you need to sell a particular product or service. Be careful with "clever" ads. Cleverness often becomes the theme of the ad, and selling gets lost in the process. In the final analysis, your advertising must produce business for you and do so cost effectively, or you need to discontinue or change your approach.

Advertising Results

If your advertising is producing adequate results, it is not an expense. However, if your advertising is not generating business, you should eliminate it or change it. Generally, each ad should return a minimum of double its cost in gross sales revenue. However, this is a broad generalization and should serve only as an approximate guideline.

In today's world, most businesses must advertise in some medium in order to survive. So the important aspect of your advertising program is the bottom line: Does it add sales and profits to your business? There are successful businesses that do not advertise at all. One example is The Body Shop International, which sells a line of natural cosmetics in over four hundred shops in thirty-four countries, producing over $300 million in sales.[7] Anita Roddick started the first Body Shop in 1976 with a $6,500 bank loan. The Body Shop relies on word-of-mouth advertising and only recently added a mail-order catalog to help sell its products.

Many professions do not advertise, and rely instead on referrals from satisfied customers. If your business is the only food market in Last Chance, Nevada, you need only to stock the shelves, hang up your sign, and price items reasonably enough to keep customers from driving eighty miles to the chain store in Bigsville.

Image or Product: What Are You Advertising?

A good advertising program is a carefully planned, budgeted program designed to produce specific results. There are two primary approaches to advertising: (1) to increase brand awareness and (2) to sell a specific product or service. Increasing awareness of a brand or a company image is usually the domain of larger companies with big bucks and chain stores with national or international markets. Look at your present advertising and determine what exactly you are trying to sell: a product or an image.

Using the Right Psychology

Your ad must speak loud and clear to a legitimate need or want. To do this, your advertising must appeal to one of the key human wants or needs: the desire to avoid some type of loss or danger or the desire to gain something—prestige, safety, health, enjoyment, comfort, money, or time. Essentially, when you approach a customer, either in person or through the advertising media, that customer is making an often subjective appraisal of the benefits that will be received in proportion to the cost.

Don Kanter, a senior advertising executive for the Chicago firm RCS&A, explains, "Every time a person is confronted with a buying decision, he will subconsciously assign a worth to the benefits he receives. At the same time, he assigns a worth to the price he has to pay. And very subjectively, very subconsciously, he divides one into the other to reach his buying decision. If, in his mind, the benefits outweigh the price . . . he will buy. If in his mind, the price outweighs the benefits . . . he will not buy." Your advertisement must convince the customer that the benefits are more than worth the price.

In the final analysis, remember that your advertising represents you and your business. Keep it honest, straightforward, and centered on benefits that help people. Be sure it is not an expense but a profit and sales generator. If not, drop it, change it, or drastically reduce it.

Ways to Make Your Advertising More Effective

To make your advertising more effective, there are tried and tested methods you should apply to your particular business.

BENEFITS VERSUS FEATURES. Your advertising must clearly describe benefits to the customer, not product features. There is a big difference. In other words, don't tell people your widget is twelve inches wide; tell them it is small enough to fit neatly on their desks. Instead of selling a tire, sell the safety that comes with the tire. You will often explain different benefits to different customers for the same product. Although safety may sell the tire to family-oriented customers, others may see more benefit in the style, performance, or economy the tire offers.

SELECTING THE RIGHT MEDIA. What will provide you the most direct route to your customers? It may be newspaper advertising, radio, direct mail, television, newsletters, magazines, catalogs, coupons, promotions, specialty publications, endorsements, or the yellow pages. You have to offer your products in the right media. If you are repairing transmissions, you would not want to place an ad in a seed catalog.

Choosing the right media to use for your advertising is a vital decision that hopefully will produce cost-effective ads for your business. First, ask yourself, "Who are my typical customers and where do they live?" For example, a French restaurant passes out a questionnaire to its customers and finds out that 65 percent of its customers are women who work within a two-and-one-half-mile radius of the restaurant. This restaurant would want to use a medium that concentrates on a specific geographic area and reaches women. However, these potential customers could also be reached at their homes, a fact that suddenly expands the media possibilities. Certain radio stations might work well or particular sections of a local newspaper of interest to women. The restaurant might advertise a special low-calorie lunch in a food supplement.

The first and most important decision in your advertising is picking out the right media. You may have a good ad that is not being seen by the right people. The services of a good ad agency may be appropriate and valuable. You should consider an agency if you do not have advertising expertise or a competent marketing and advertising staff in your company. In a reorganization, a good agency can be a real time saver for you, enabling you to concentrate on other matters. Remember that effective advertising will more than pay for any fees charged by an ad agency. However, if you decide to use an agency, get several competitive bids and work within a specified budget. Some agencies think money grows on trees and will spend yours like lightning if you do not give them clear and definite dollar limits.

The most common method used to compare the cost of different media is the *cost per thousand,* or CPM. The cost per thousand is found with the following formula:

$$\text{Cost per thousand} = \frac{\text{Your actual advertising cost}}{\text{Circulation or delivered audience}} \times 1{,}000$$

By comparing the cost per thousand for different media, you will see what it is actually costing you per potential customer. However, when using this method, be careful you are comparing apples with apples. As an example, a radio station may have a large number of listeners and a seemingly very low per person advertising cost, but only a tiny percentage of those listeners may actually be potential customers; a product for senior citizens would not sell on a hard rock station, whereas an ad in a senior citizen magazine with a much smaller audience and a higher per person ad cost might produce excellent sales results.

TRACKING RESULTS. Develop a method for tracking ad results. Be sure each ad is producing tangible returns. A simple method of tracking results from advertising is to ask the customer to do something that ties the sale to the ad. Part of the ad might say, "Mention this ad and receive a bonus gift." Including a coupon is a direct way to measure ad response. Each ad can be keyed by assigning unique product numbers or names to items in the ad, or the ad itself can be keyed if it requires the customer to mail or call in an order. For example, the order address can start with "Dept. L410," meaning the ad is in the April 10 *Los Angeles Times.* Another way to track ad results is to ask customers how they heard about your store or why they stopped by. The answers can be noted by employees on a card kept at checkout stations or cash registers as customers purchase goods.

To accurately track ad results, you need to know the following: (1) where the ad was placed (what media); (2) the date(s) of issue; (3) the number of insertions; (4) the cost of the ad; (5) item(s) advertised; (6) the number of inquiries; (7) the number of orders; and (8) total dollar sales. If your advertising is geared to building your image as opposed to selling specific products, it will be difficult to track the results (see Appendix A for advertising and marketing aids). If you have assigned key numbers to several ads, you can compare these data to determine which ads yielded the most sales.

How to Promote Word-of-Mouth Advertising

Word-of-mouth advertising is especially important to a small business and can be an extremely effective way to increase sales without direct advertising. A satisfied and happy customer is always your best advertisement. An unhappy customer can be devastating to your business.

Gregory Passewitz, a small-business specialist for Ohio State University, explains, "Word-of-mouth advertising is so important, especially to a small business. Conversely, negative word-of-mouth can be devastating. Some recent surveys show that when people are upset (with a company), they tell nine or ten people about it. When they're happy, they tell about five."[8]

Promoting word-of-mouth advertising means you need to have a method of measuring customer satisfaction that is reliable and timely. Teach your employees to *listen* with respect and genuine interest to customers—both complaints and praise. Make it a clear company policy that customers come first, that without customers there is no business. Let customers know as soon as possible that you are aware of their presence. As an example, a restaurant server may be busy, but someone can immediately greet patrons, bring a glass of water, and let them know someone will be coming to take their order. Without this kind of simple acknowledgment, anger and frustration soon dominate customers' feelings, and you may never see them again.

Seeding a Market

Apple is probably the most well-known company that has profitably used the marketing technique of seeding a market by giving away thousands of Apple computers to school systems and has built a bond between the company and hundreds of thousands of potential future customers. The result today is that Apple has almost become a standard product in the nation's school systems. Another company, Lotus Development Corporation, gives away products to influential company executives, who, having used and liking its product, become another sales force for Lotus.

A Salt Lake City–based company went from start-up to over $52 million in annual sales in six years. Its training and time management courses are often introduced to potential corporate clients through seminars. The company invites several executives from other companies (at no charge) to its seminars when it is conducting on-site programs for a particular company. If these executives like the products, experience shows that they will often become future customers of the company.[9]

The Hazard of Increased Sales

In considering advertising, the question arises, "Should you increase sales at all?" Rapid growth can be fatal. Big sales increases may very well be the cause of your financial difficulties. A common situation in a rapidly growing business is a cash flow crunch caused by increasing inventory and accounts receivable. Inventory-intensiveness and a large percentage of charge account business are often a deadly combination. A business owner finds it necessary to obtain large new infusions of cash to finance the escalating inventory and receivables to sustain the sales growth. One of the solutions may be to put a brake on rapidly increasing sales until your cash flow catches up.

Saving your business may require dropping certain product lines or some other form of retrenching to put the breaks on out-of-control sales increases. I worked recently with a company whose sales were increasing so fast that the owner was having difficulty financing the growing inventory and the enormous increase in accounts receivable. He was caught in a real cash squeeze, but he was also caught in the excitement of rapidly increasing sales and kept adding sales people to sell still more products and some new product lines. Eventually he had to cut back the sales force and discontinue certain products so that the business could stabilize itself financially.

Uncountable companies have failed from the inability to finance the inventory and accounts receivable resulting from rapid sales increases. However, if your sales are on the decline, your marketing strategies and advertising plans must be an important aspect of your reorganization plans. If your sales are decreasing, you need to change something: management, service, quality, advertising, marketing, decor, image. Find out what other successful companies in your field are doing.

Checklist Points

1. Review your marketing program from start to finish. Determine its weak points and strong points. Evolve a strategy that eliminates the weak areas and builds on the strong points.
2. Make sure you are doing everything possible to keep your existing customers. Personally review customer complaints to

find areas that need improvement. Design a system suitable for your business to get customer feedback on quality, service, price, and treatment by your employees.

3. Eliminate advertising unless it is cost-effective, or change it so that it is cost-effective. Advertising that is not producing added sales is a big cash drain. Don't advertise anything without some way to track the results accurately.

Staying on Track

Who does not guard his enterprise until he gains his goal, often is taken by surprise that robs him of the whole.
                              —Lao-tsu

Follow Up Your Progress

Once you have decided how to reorganize your business to generate more profit, you must develop systems to follow up on the progress of your plans. Set definite time deadlines for each phase and step. Having a complete system in place for tracking the progress of your reorganization is essential and will ensure your success. Proper implementation and follow-up will ensure that your business will stay on track.

Employees

Keep employees informed of the company's progress through regularly planned meetings, thus preventing speculation and anxiety regarding the future of your business and their jobs.

Make sure that the goals you set for your employees are realistic. It is far better to proceed in increments, setting objectives and goals that can be met. You must find a balance between what is impossible and what amounts to no change at all. A goal should create tension: it should challenge one's ingenuity but be attainable.

At this point, you need to make sure your employees are being fairly compensated for their efforts. If they are meeting their goals, employees should be seeing some tangible benefits: bonuses, pay increases, or other compensation or recognition for a job well done. Before hiring any new people, should your situation warrant it, try to get by with temporary help until the cost of temporary help is consistently higher than the expense of hiring a full-time employee. In short, be very conservative and cautious when it comes to adding permanent employees to your staff. Until your business is firmly established on solid financial ground with a good track record of sustained sales and profits, you should resist adding any new personnel.

Setting Up a Monitoring System

You should establish a schedule to monitor your company's vital statistics as an ongoing check on the progress of your reorganization efforts. Use the following procedure as a guideline to set up your own system.

Review on a daily basis:

- Daily cash and sales status report (Exhibit 8.3)
- Customer complaints and feedback

Review on a weekly basis:

- Accounts receivable aging (Exhibit 8.4)
- Accounts payable aging
- Collections and average age of receivables in days
- Follow-up of collection efforts on past-due accounts
- Purchases-to-date compared with sales-to-date
- Advertising results

Review on a monthly basis:

- Cash flow variance report (Exhibit 8.2)
- Comparative income statement (this year/last year)
- Gross profit margins
- Payroll expense
- Sales increase/decrease to date
- Operating expenses this year and last year
- Any increases in expense
- Expense increases in *percentage of total sales*
- Balance sheet and statement of changes in financial position
- Ratio of current assets to current liabilities

- Ratio of total assets to total liabilities
- Accounts receivable; compare aging with last month
- Accounts payable: compare aging with last month
- Inventory status; compare this month with last month
- Changes in financial assets: cash, receivables, and liabilities

Predicting Your Future: Monthly Cash Flow Projections

You are now at the stage where you can plan a three-month cash flow projection. You should always have your operations planned for at least three months ahead, or six months if possible. Remember to be realistic in all your planning and projections. It is well established that unrealistic or unattainable goals will quickly undermine your plans because your employees will feel frustrated in attempting to meet objectives that cannot be met.

Look over Exhibit 8.1 and follow this format for your new plans. Estimate, as realistically as possible, your sales, expenses, and profits for the next three-month period. This estimate will give you target numbers to check against your actual results each month. The simplest way to do this is with a cash flow variance as in Exhibit 8.2. A budget variance shows the dollar difference between your projected budget and your actual operations.

Verifying Results

Actually checking your results each month is extremely important. Any significant budget variance will alert you to necessary additional cutbacks before things get out of hand. Review Able Company's figures for their projected cash flow and its variance. You can easily prepare this report yourself, or you may have your bookkeeper or accountant prepare it for you. Remember that in all our cash flow reports we are dealing only with *cash* items, not depreciation or any other paper expenses.

Daily Status Reports

The daily status report (Exhibit 8.3) was developed for a restaurant in order to give the owner a daily picture of the cash position of his

Able Company Cash Flow Projection	Period: 6/1/92 thru 8/31/92		
	June	July	August
BEGINNING CASH	$8,482	$14,071	$23,738
ADD: CASH RECEIPTS	$79,500	$80,750	$82,600
TOTAL CASH AVAILABLE	$87,982	$94,821	$106,338
EXPENSES:			
Purchases for Resale	$23,850	$26,648	$28,910
Payments to Creditors	7.660	7,660	7,660
Rent: Building & Equipment	5,500	2,500	2,500
Salaries	18,000	17,000	15,750
Executive Salaries	2,500	2,500	2,500
Payroll Taxes	2,460	2,340	2,190
Fringe Benefits	1,282	985	985
Accounting & Legal	1,200	1,500	1,750
Advertising	1,600	1,250	985
Office Supplies & Postage	195	200	200
Insurance	1,250	795	795
Utilities	750	800	850
Operating Supplies	3,180	3,230	3,304
Telephone	694	700	725
Auto Expense	688	700	695
Miscellaneous	176	180	195
Bank Loan (Principal)	1,667	1,667	1,667
Bank Loan (Interest)	830	0	0
Other Loans	429	429	429
TOTAL CASH PAID OUT	$73,911	$71,084	$72,090
NET CASH FLOW	$5,589	$9,667	$10,510
ENDING CASH	$14,071	$23,738	$34,248

EXHIBIT 8.1

business. It is an excellent way to alert you to sudden changes and trends that need corrective measures before they become unmanageable. The most important items to track are payroll expense, accounts receivable aging, purchases, inventory, cash flow, and sales revenue. Variances in any of these categories will have immediate consequences for your reorganization plan and should result in instant remedial action on your part.

Exhibit 8.4 is a weekly accounts receivable status report that gives you vital information about the age of your receivables and the change from week to week. This type of report enables you to spot a trend

Able Company Cash Flow Variance	Month: July-92		
	Budget	Actual	Variance
BEGINNING CASH	$8,482	$13,653	$5,171
ADD: CASH RECEIPTS	$79,500	$80,750	$1,250
TOTAL CASH AVAILABLE	$87,982	$94,403	$6,421
EXPENSES:			
Purchases for Resale	$24,750	$26,648	$1,898
Payments to Creditors	7,660	7,660	0
Rent: Building & Equipment	5,500	2,500	(3,000)
Salaries	18,000	18,250	250
Executive Salaries	2,500	3,500	1,000
Payroll Taxes	2,460	2,610	150
Fringe Benefits	900	1,182	282
Accounting & Legal	1,350	1,500	150
Advertising	1,600	1,250	(350)
Office Supplies & Postage	195	135	(60)
Insurance	1,000	910	(90)
Utilities	750	800	50
Operating Supplies	3,180	3,230	50
Telephone	694	715	21
Auto Expense	688	720	32
Miscellaneous	176	180	4
Bank Loan (Principal)	1,667	1,667	0
Bank Loan (Interest)	830	0	(830)
Other Loans	429	429	0
TOTAL CASH PAID OUT	$74,329	$73,886	($444)
NET CASH FLOW	$5,171	$6,865	$1,694
ENDING CASH	$13,653	$20,518	$6,865

EXHIBIT 8.2

before it mushrooms and take corrective action immediately. Receivables are often a company's biggest source of cash and must be given high priority in your reorganization plans.

Crisis Prevention

Setting up an early warning system is an important preventive measure. By now you are probably an expert on business problems, but

Daily Cash/Sales Status Report	Date: 5-24-92

Bank Balances (Operating Cash):

Operating Account	$13,867
Payroll Account	4,421
Combined Balance (After deducting payments)	18,288
Money Mkt. Funds - Reserve	28,191
CD - Reserve	30,443
Total Cash Resources	**$76,922**

Payments Thru: 5-24-92

Sales Taxes: 5-20	$3,778
Payroll Transfer: 5-21	6,000
Misc. Bills: 5-22	1,696
FICA/FIT Tax Deposit: 5-24	2,344
Total Payments	**$13,818**

Daily Sales Report: Sales Thru 5-24-92

Total Sales to Date:	$40,622	1992 Sales/Day:	$1,766
Projected for Month:	$54,752	1991 Sales/Day:	$1,856
Estimated Inc./Dec.:	-$2,799	1991 Actual:	$57,551
Percent Inc/Dec:	-4.86		
Cash Over/Short	$22.07		

EXHIBIT 8.3

it is a good idea to keep in mind the signs that forewarn that trouble is ahead. Here are the most important warning signs:

- Profits on a downward trend
- Inability to pay any bills on time
- Increased borrowing on receivables, inventory, or other assets
- Deteriorating employee morale
- Sales in a continued state of decline
- Liabilities increasing as a percentage of sales
- Cash shortages
- Problems meeting payroll or paying taxes

When you recognize one of these warning signs in your business, don't make a mistake that will compound the problem. Following these principles will help to keep you out of trouble:

1. Avoid borrowing money as a remedy for cash shortages. Cash flow problems should be handled by correcting the specific business operations that are causing the problems. Look at receivables, col-

Accounts Receivable Status Report: 5-24-92			
Current Week:		**Prior Week:**	
Amount: 0-30 Days:	$60,000	0-30 Days:	$50,000
Amount: 31-60 Days:	20,000	31-60 Days:	25,000
Amount: 61-90 Days:	15,000	61-90 Days:	27,500
Amount: 91 + Days:	5,000	91 + Days:	17,500
Total A/R:	**$100,000**	**Total A/R:**	**$120,000**
A/R Age: Days:	51	A/R Age: Days:	61

EXHIBIT 8.4

lections, purchases, inventory, and any increasing expenses. Avoid any high-leverage investments for your business or yourself. High leverage is always a higher risk.

2. Establish a cash emergency fund. Set up a systematic savings plan, and set aside these funds in a CD or other savings account. Use this fund only for emergency or unforeseen events. Replenish it as soon as possible if you do draw out funds.

3. Be conservative and make it a practice not to be drawn into spending with the business cycles. This means that when times are good, you should take advantage of the situation by saving more or paying off some debts or bank loans.

4. Do not purchase anything that has high monthly payments. In business, it is tempting to lease new equipment without really looking into the total cost involved. It is often much better to pay cash for something as opposed to leasing for four or five years with high payments and interest. However, do not make a cash purchase that will adversely affect your day-to-day operating capital.

5. Be careful to monitor what your customers want, through questionnaires, phone calls, business reply cards, or some regular system that works for your business. Make it a policy to consistently study your customers' needs, and especially their complaints about your service or products.

6. Don't load up your business with employees or fringe benefits in good times that may have to be eliminated in a down cycle. Make

it a policy never to add benefits that you do not intend to be a permanent expense.

7. Maintain a monthly budget to monitor cash flow, sales, and operating expenses. Never let these important business tools slip into misuse. Also develop a contingency budget plan that anticipates a recession—a 30 or 40 percent drop in business.

8. Be sure you maintain up-to-date monthly, comparative financial statements and that the information is reviewed and action taken where necessary.

9. Carry the minimum business and personal insurance that will protect you from a disaster or sudden illness. Investigate business interruption insurance, but watch the expense involved and weigh the risk factor for your particular type of business. Also check into personal disability insurance that will provide a minimum of 50 percent of your salary for twenty-four months if you are unable to perform your normal job duties. Don't risk losing everything you've worked for because you're underinsured or have no insurance. Disability insurance is often bypassed by small business owners, but premiums are generally small and can be designed to suit your particular needs and situation. Insurance planners recommend that, in order to avoid being taxed on the benefits, you pay for the premiums out of personal funds. If your business pays for the premiums and then deducts them as an expense, you personally have to pay taxes on the benefits. Exhibit 8-5 shows the estimated disability insurance premiums for a small business owner who is thirty-five, owns a retail store, and does some supervisory work. The premiums are for a policy that pays benefits until age sixty-five.

10. Have a specific plan on how to survive personally for at least six months should you be unable to draw a salary. You should set

Disability Insurance Premiums	
Annual Premium	**Monthly Benefit**
$784	$1,850
$1,359	$3,300
$1,955	$4,800

Source: New York Life Insurance Co., August, 1992

EXHIBIT 8.5

aside funds for these possibilities or have a plan to obtain cash for emergency situations.

11. Make sure you have legally provided for the disposition or continuation of your business in the event of your illness or death. Have a buy/sell agreement drawn up, and review it on an annual basis. A buy/sell agreement is a legal document that provides for a specific way to continue or sell all or part of a business in the event of a crisis, or in case a partner or shareholder wants to buy or sell a share of the business. Your attorney and accountant should be consulted to prepare a buy/sell agreement that is tailored to your particular business needs.

12. Don't let yourself become complacent. Always be in the process of exploring new approaches, new markets, and creative and innovative ways to sell your products or services.

PART THREE

Declaring Bankruptcy

The recession, coupled with the vast amount of debt accumulated in the 1980s, has taken its toll across the U.S. Business failures increased in every region of the country last year (1991) and in every major U.S. industry, from services to manufacturing.
   —*Joseph Duncan, economist for Dun & Bradstreet, March 1992*

The Bankruptcy Path

A record 944,000 American individuals and businesses filed for bankruptcy in 1991—a 21% increase from the year before. It was the highest number since the current U.S. Bankruptcy code took effect in 1979 and the seventh consecutive increase nationally.
                    —The American Bankruptcy Institute

Business failures are setting record levels. There were 87,266 business failures in the United States in 1991, a 43.7 percent increase over 1990. Unpaid debts totaled an incredible $108.8 billion in 1991, a 95.9 percent increase over 1990. Debt-burdened businesses, personal debt, tighter credit, and failed leveraged buyouts contributed to the rise of bankruptcy rates.[1] Dun & Bradstreet compiled the following statistics on the causes of business failures:

- Insufficient profits, 22.2 percent
- Poor growth, 19.8 percent
- Too much debt or too little capital, 14.7 percent
- Inexperience, 12.0 percent
- Heavy operating expenses, 11.7 percent
- Industry weakness, 10.5 percent
- High interest rates, poor location, competition, 5.3 percent
- Neglect, 2.0 percent
- Fraud, 0.9 percent
- Poor planning, 0.9 percent

One of the three major causes of business failure is debt, because of the generally fixed nature of principal and interest payments that must be met in spite of the inevitable economic cycles and fluctuations in the business world. A large amount of debt in a business acts as an undermining drain on the operations, resulting in lower profit margins, higher operating costs, and *much greater risk* when business slows down.

Debt gives you leverage in two directions: up and down. Leverage is determined by the ratio of debt to total assets: zero debt means zero leverage. For example, a business purchases a competitor and finances the purchase by issuing bonds (debt). If the new business venture does well, generating enough profits to cover the interest payments on the bonds plus additional profits, all goes well. Such a situation is the use of leverage to gain control over assets with a minimum or, in our example, zero investment—100 percent financing. However, the risk is multiplied during economic slumps. Then a business finds it impossible to meet interest payments, triggering a default and potential bankruptcy. This is how debt leverages, or multiplies, the benefits in good times but also sinks the financial boat much more quickly in bad times.

A well-known business that was in bankruptcy is the Manville Corporation. It was forced into Chapter 11 bankruptcy by lawsuits totaling billions of dollars over health damage caused by asbestos fiber. It filed bankruptcy in 1982 to protect itself from the mounting legal claims, even though it was a highly profitable company. Six years after its bankruptcy filing, Manville emerged from Chapter 11 under a complex and creative reorganization plan that set up an independent trust, funded by the company's profits, which will eventually provide about $3 billion to asbestos injury victims over the next thirty years.[2] This is a good example of how a Chapter 11 plan can really save a company even in seemingly impossible circumstances.

If a reorganization of your business fails, bankruptcy may be your only alternative. In this chapter, we will look at the different bankruptcy procedures. It is not within the scope of the book to elaborate on the specific mechanics of filing bankruptcy. However, I will attempt to give you a good overview of the options available to you and also hopefully answer some of the questions you probably have regarding bankruptcy proceedings and the consequences of filing bankruptcy. I do not intend this book to take the place of competent legal advice. You must be the judge of what legal help is needed in your unique situation and when. Filing bankruptcy is a step that should be undertaken only with serious and careful consideration of the consequences both to you as an individual, to your family, and to your business. If you decide to try filing bankruptcy without an attorney, you can get blank forms at any legal stationery store, and usually from the bankruptcy court clerk.

What Is Bankruptcy?

A bankruptcy is a legal process that relieves a debtor of all or part of his or her debts. Bankruptcy proceedings are designed to give an individual or business a fresh start and at the same time to give fair treatment to all creditors. An individual, corporation, or partnership can voluntarily declare bankruptcy. Insolvency is not a requirement for bankruptcy, but you may not use the bankruptcy laws for fraudulent purposes. You should consider bankruptcy only as a last resort, and only after you have exhausted all other options in straightening out your financial affairs.

In most cases the assets and property of a debtor are turned over to a trustee, frequently a private attorney, appointed by the court. These assets are then converted into cash by the trustee and distributed to the creditors who have filed claims against the individual or business that filed bankruptcy. For an individual bankruptcy, you must submit a list of creditors and a schedule of assets and liabilities; prepare a statement of your affairs; surrender all books, property, and records to the trustee; appear at all hearings involving the granting of a discharge; and attend all creditor meetings.

Both a husband and a wife should file bankruptcy if most debts are owned jointly, and if most property and assets are owned jointly. If only one individual files bankruptcy, the other may end up paying all the debts. Either husband or wife can file bankruptcy independently. However, if they file a joint petition, only one filing fee needs to be paid. Separate filing should be considered only after determining the consequences of joint ownership of assets and property.

There are two basic types of bankruptcies: a *reorganization* and a *liquidation.*

Reorganization

Reorganization differs from liquidation in that all debts, along with a plan for payment of all debts, are turned over to the bankruptcy court. The court then immediately issues an order preventing your creditors from all attempts to collect from you. A reorganization enables you to make regular payments to the trustee, who then distributes the funds to your creditors under a court-approved plan. The court approves an individual plan to repay each creditor.

Liquidation

In a liquidation, all one's assets (except for exempt property) are sold or liquidated, and the proceeds are apportioned to all creditors based on priority as set by law. In this form of bankruptcy, all nonexempt assets are given to a trustee appointed by the court. Creditors are then paid only out of the proceeds from the sale (usually at auction) of nonexempt assets. The debtor (the individual or business that files bankruptcy) is discharged of all of the eligible claims of the creditors (those firms or individuals whom he or she owes money). Certain types of debt are nondischargeable—exempt.

Business Bankruptcy Options

Chapter 11 Reorganization

Chapter 11 reorganization is a rehabilitation plan to pay off your creditors that must be approved by the court. Under this plan, a business continues to operate while putting together a plan to pay off creditors over an extended period of time at reduced prices. You negotiate with creditors and shareholders and put together a workable plan, which is then presented to the court. When the court officially approves or confirms the plan, you must then follow the plan as to the payments and other arrangements made. Your business debts are totally discharged as long as you follow the terms of the plan. This plan commonly includes reorganizing a company's debt structure, moratoriums on interest, deferred or reduced payments, the sale of certain assets, and any other restructuring necessary. A Chapter 11 plan can be filed by a business or individual debtor, but it is rarely used by individuals due to the expense and complex nature of the proceeding.

A petition must be filed with the court that explains in detail your financial affairs and your potential for eventual recovery. Once this petition is filed, your business is legally protected from creditors. A typical Chapter 11 plan takes from nine to twelve months to make its way through all the court proceedings, just to get the petition approved. A business can remain in a Chapter 11 reorganization for many years. In fact, 50 percent of all the Chapter 11 cases filed since 1979 are still unresolved.[3]

ADVANTAGES. A Chapter 11 proceeding protects you from collection efforts by your creditors so that you have time to develop a plan to pay your debts. All legal proceedings against your business are stopped, including any lawsuits or judgments. You remain in business but must operate under very strict legal restraints. Depending on your particular situation, the court may appoint a trustee to operate your business and disburse all payments to creditors. A reorganization enables businesses to keep their property while installment payments are made by the trustee (court-appointed) to the various creditors.

This approach is desirable when you have valuable assets that you feel are vital to the continuation of your business and you also have an income sufficient to sustain your business. This plan essentially gives you extra time to pay your debts while legally stopping creditor collection attempts and lawsuits.

Interest payments on your unsecured debts are suspended during the proceedings and do not have to be repaid later. Payments to creditors (secured and unsecured) can be extended, reduced, or changed in any manner that facilitates the reorganization. All claims are consolidated and taken care of in the one bankruptcy case.

You are entitled to make decisions for the benefit of your company. You can streamline and revamp management, shutdown unprofitable operations, and sell any assets needed to help your cash flow. However, if the court places a trustee in charge of your business, your ability to make many decisions will be restricted. You continue to operate your business while being legally protected from creditors and any collection attempts. Lawsuits in progress at the time of the filing are frozen (stayed). Your business is rehabilitated and given a fresh start so that you can eventually repay your debts.

DISADVANTAGES. A drawback to a Chapter 11 reorganization is the fact that often a court-appointed trustee takes charge of the operations of the business and concentrates solely on the income and distribution of funds. A business in financial straits also needs expert marketing and operational help during the recovery process, which trustees usually have no time to give. In your business, a Chapter 11 proceeding will hurt your business reputation and demolish the value of your stock, especially if it is publicly traded.

Chapter 11's primary drawbacks are the likelihood of considerable legal expense and damage to your credibility as a reputable business person. In this type of proceeding, most creditors are not repaid the full amounts owed.

Chapter 11 proceedings can be complex and expensive, especially for a small business. Ironically, there are many businesses that cannot afford to file a Chapter 11 plan. The filing fee for a Chapter 11 is $200. These fees do not include attorney's fees, which range from $500 on up. Attorney fees for a Chapter 11 bankruptcy normally start around $2,000. Even the smallest business can expect to pay about $10,000 for a simple Chapter 11 filing. A business Chapter 11 reorganization can cost tens of thousands of dollars depending on the complexity of the particular business.

Another drawback is that very few Chapter 11 companies recover. Chapter 11 is supposed to be a way to rehabilitate a business, eventually making it a viable and profitable enterprise in the community. However, statistics reveal that only a small minority of companies actually survive a Chapter 11 reorganization, and that 88 to 90 percent go out of business,[4] often after many years of delay and enormous legal fees. It is commonly only very large businesses with plenty of cash or salable assets that make it through the Chapter 11 process. Even the companies that survive often bear little resemblance to the business that entered bankruptcy. Assets are sold off, people fired, plants closed, and products discontinued, and top management is usually replaced with new people brought in from outside the company.

A New Chapter 11 Alternative

Many companies are now opting for "prepackaged" bankruptcies rather than traditional Chapter 11 proceedings. In a prepackaged plan, you make a deal with your creditors before filing a petition, greatly increasing the probability of survival of your business, and your business is still protected under the Chapter 11 code. You present all creditors, lenders, and equity shareholders with a reorganization plan before the bankruptcy filing goes to court. Under bankruptcy law, more than 50 percent of your creditors must accept your plan—and within each class of creditors, the approving votes must account for at least two thirds of the amount of claims (creditors are segregated into two basic classes: secured and unsecured). Because of these regulations, it is a good idea to test a sampling of your creditors to be sure you can get the required votes. A prepackaged plan can make a Chapter 11 a totally different ball game, and it may save your business.

A prepackaged plan includes a disclosure statement with all pertinent details, both positive and negative, about your company's finances. Then, all parties concerned resolve their differences and agree to the plan, which generally describes how the business will be reorganized to operate more efficiently, who will manage it, and exactly what resources will be needed to accomplish the plan. This plan also gives details about any debt restructuring and how it will be done.[5]

A business must have the real potential for recovery to benefit from a prepackaged plan. If you do not have a viable business operation to start with, a prepackaged plan will offer no advantages over the traditional Chapter 11. A prepackaged plan will still need approval by a bankruptcy judge, but you won't have to start the negotiation process again in the courts, so you will save the added expense of court-appointed creditor committees and professional fees. With a prepackaged plan, your business shows creditors and bankers up-front that it can operate successfully while meeting its financial obligations according to the agreed-upon plan.

ADVANTAGES. A prepackaged deal can be completed in four to nine months as opposed to one to two years or more for the traditional process. Prepackaged bankruptcy plans offer a much faster resolution of creditors' claims, and once a plan is agreed upon by a majority of creditors, it can be used as leverage to convince other reluctant ones. Even if some creditors reject the plan, they are bound by the majority vote when the court confirms the prepackaged plan. This new technique combines the speediness of an out-of-court settlement with the protection of Chapter 11. A prepackaged plan provides a much more stable environment in which to work out differences than the typical bankruptcy court. Most lenders prefer to negotiate on their own behalf as opposed to having their interests controlled by the bankruptcy court. In addition, bankers may be more willing to provide additional funds if you already have creditors' agreement to a debt-restructuring package.

A prepackaged plan restores lender confidence. Lenders like prepackaged plans because of the minimizing of the legal expense, the usual long delays, and the unpredictability in working out a traditional Chapter 11 plan. Creditors also like to avoid the confrontational aspect of the traditional Chapter 11 approach. When delays are reduced, the legal and accounting expenses involved in a reorganization are also reduced—and creditors save the similar legal and accounting expenses normally incurred in protracted negotiations.

The adverse business effects of a normal Chapter 11 are minimized, and the Chapter 11 filing becomes a much more predictable, and therefore surmountable, process. Often, with a traditional Chapter 11, creditors and lenders do not hear about a bankruptcy until the bankruptcy is filed with the court. As a result, the confidence of a company's creditors and lenders plummets. Many times a secured lender will liquidate the collateral to get its money back; creditors and competitors will be quick to capitalize on a company's financial troubles. Long-standing customers and suppliers usually disappear, adding difficulties for your business.

With a prepackaged plan, you can avoid often unpredictable and lengthy legal battles by coming to terms with creditors before legal proceedings even begin. The less time spent in bankruptcy proceedings, the greater will be the chance of eventual recovery.

DISADVANTAGES. There are some drawbacks to a prepackaged Chapter 11. Notifying creditors about a reorganization plan sends warning signals into the business community that there is trouble brewing. This can trigger a forced, premature bankruptcy filing, and the business may quickly lose control of the situation.

There are potential legal problems when a business asks for creditors' votes outside the normal court process. If there is any misrepresentation in your disclosure statement, you will expose yourself to extensive and expensive legal battles and probably ruin the entire plan. A definite risk is attached to a prepackaged approach, and all potential problems must be realistically examined before a plan is launched. The best way to reduce these risks is to hire the best expert legal and professional counsel you can find. Competent advisers will also help you hold onto as much equity in your business as is possible under the circumstances. If you are interested in a prepackaged plan, you will definitely need legal help experienced in this approach to bankruptcy.

Chapter 7 Liquidation

Chapter 7 is a complete liquidation of all your business assets. Often this plan will force a Chapter 7 personal bankruptcy as well if you have personally guaranteed loans or notes for your business. If your business is not incorporated, you are personally liable for all debts. A business or an individual can file a Chapter 7 plan. The result, a liquidation of assets, is the same. A business chooses a Chapter 7 liquidation only if the prospects of salvaging the business are zero, and there is no desire or means on the part of the owner to undertake a reorganization. The same consideration is true for an individual. Most individuals who file Chapter 7 liquidations do not have any substantial assets and simply want to get a fresh start. Even in a liquidation, there are certain exempt assets that can be kept by an individual, but most exemptions do not apply to a business Chapter 7.

ADVANTAGES. A Chapter 7 liquidation can be done very quickly; two to three months from beginning to end is not uncommon. Speed is definitely an advantage when you are in very dire financial circumstances. Legal expenses are minimized in this approach, for both a business and an individual. Legal expenses for a small business can start as low as $500. Once the assets are sold, legal expenses are over. At the time of this writing, there is a filing fee of $120 for a Chapter 7 liquidation. All debts are discharged with one legal filing. Creditors cannot harass you, and all legal and collection activity is stopped the moment a petition is filed. However, a Chapter 7 does not exempt you from paying all federal and state taxes owed. In addition, all customer deposits must be returned.

Under a Chapter 7 liquidation, your business is closed, all property is sold, and the remains, if any, after paying legal fees and sales commissions are distributed to your creditors by a court-appointed or supervised trustee.

DISADVANTAGES. The primary disadvantage is that you lose everything, not only your business and all its assets, but your job, credit rating, and most business acquaintances who were your "friends" as long as you were a good customer and doing well. You'll realize very quickly that there is a definite stigma associated with bankruptcy—and the worst stigma comes from a Chapter 7 liquidation because, basically, no one gets paid unless you are liquidating substantial and valuable assets. In fact, it is not at all uncommon to see former business suppliers become bitter enemies. They will feel that you have betrayed their trust, and they will be angry! You and your family may have to deal with the emotional repercussions for a long time after the bankruptcy is over.

When you file a Chapter 7 liquidation, certain creditors can try to stop the filing, especially if they feel any assets have been disposed of illegally just before the action was filed. Bankers often want to scrutinize the financial information you have given them. If they find any misleading financial numbers, they can initiate expensive legal proceedings against the owner of the business and potentially exempt themselves from being discharged as creditors. This means you will still have to pay the bank loans.

After the dust has settled, usually at an auction, you'll be lucky to get ten cents on the dollar for your business assets, and you receive payment only if there is a surplus left after paying all creditors, which is highly unlikely!

Only the debts you formally list can be discharged. This way you can continue the use of a credit card if needed for special situations such as car rentals or travel reservations. This is true for both businesses and individuals. If you have some particular bills or charge accounts you still want to use, do not list them as debtors in your petition. However, be careful you don't violate the bankruptcy laws that prevent you from giving preferential payments to certain creditors. Signing a false bankruptcy petition or schedules is a federal crime, punishable by fines as well as imprisonment.

Involuntary Proceedings

Often creditors do favor a bankruptcy because it generally ensures them equitable treatment by the court. Without bankruptcy, a debtor can give preferential treatment to certain creditors. It is possible for creditors to force an individual or business into bankruptcy, but only in special circumstances. There must be more than eleven creditors, and there must be three or more creditors with total debt of at least $5,000. This debt amount of $5,000 must be over and above the value of any lien on any property securing the creditors' claims. The general requirement is simply the demonstrated inability of the debtor or business to pay its bills when they are due.

Businesses do have some protection from wrongful involuntary bankruptcy proceedings. A bankruptcy court has the power to dismiss an involuntary proceeding or to suspend all proceedings, especially if the court believes that other means are available to settle the dispute between a debtor and a creditor.

Courts will award debtors damages, including loss of business and punitive damages, if an involuntary bankruptcy case is wrongfully filed by creditors. The court will also require the creditors to pay all legal and court costs of the debtor in the case of a filing in bad faith by one's creditors.

Employees of a firm are generally excluded from joining in an involuntary petition. Although employees cannot initiate involuntary bankruptcy proceedings, claims for unpaid wages or payments owed to retirement plans become first-priority claims in a Chapter 11 or Chapter 7 business bankruptcy. There are special requirements for partnerships. Farmers and certain nonprofit organizations are exempt from involuntary bankruptcy proceedings. There are other technical aspects to an involuntary proceeding. If you are concerned about the possibility of a group of creditors filing an involuntary petition, be sure to get competent legal advice regarding your particular situation

Role of the Trustee

The trustee in a bankruptcy proceeding is appointed by the court to take charge of the process of the collection, sale, and distribution of the debtor's property. The trustee is responsible for all property received and can examine all claims to make sure they are valid. The trustee makes the final accounting of the estate to the court. For individual bankruptcies, the trustee's responsibilities include

1. Converting all of the debtor's assets to cash (except exempt property).
2. Investigating the financial affairs of the debtor.

3. Being accountable for all property received.
4. Making sure all the creditors' claims are valid and correct.
5. In certain circumstances, in the case of fraud or for other misrepresentation by the debtor, opposing the discharge of a debtor.
6. Furnishing reports about the debtor's business if it is authorized to be operated by the court.
7. Making a final accounting and report to the court.

In a business bankruptcy, the trustee's role is greatly expanded. In a Chapter 11 reorganization, the court usually appoints a trustee to operate the business in the interim period while a definite reorganization plan is being drawn up. The trustee, after a thorough analysis of the finances of the business, reports to the court as to the potential for recovery. The trustee also assesses the management's character and ability to go on with the business.

Once a trustee enters the scene, the former management becomes just that: former. The trustee is the "boss," making all operational and financial decisions, including the firing and hiring of employees. The trustee's authority extends to deciding whether or not to continue the business or close it down. The trustee has total authority to sell any assets or close segments of a business. The trustee's recommendations to the court are often the major factor influencing the court in its decision to confirm a reorganization plan.

Exempt and Nonexempt Property

Exempt and nonexempt property are important issues for an individual filing bankruptcy. Generally, in a business liquidation, there are no exempt assets. However, for the individual, the federal bankruptcy statutes do provide for certain property and assets of the individual to be exempt, meaning that the debtor can keep certain assets or allowable interests in certain assets and not turn them over to the bankruptcy trustee.

If a debtor receives an inheritance, money or property, or life insurance proceeds at any time within 180 days after filing the petition, everything becomes part of the bankruptcy estate. After 180 days, everything goes to the debtor free and clear of all claims. In community property states, all community property goes into the bankruptcy proceedings and is liquidated, whether the spouse files or not. In states where there are no community property statutes, only the debtor's interest becomes part of the bankruptcy estate.

In California, the federal exemption system cannot be used. A debtor must choose between two state exemption systems. However, one of the state systems is really the equivalent of the federal system. For an individual, state laws also regulate exempt property. Many states have now elected to use their own exemptions instead of the federal exemptions. You can easily check your state's laws at your local library. As an example, California law allows homeowners filing under Chapter 7 to keep up to $75,000 in home equity if they are married, $50,000 if they are single, and $100,000 if they are over 65 or disabled. There is a $1,200 equity exemption for autos. Renters can claim personal property exemptions up to $7,900.

The Federal Bankruptcy Law demands that all nonexempt assets be turned over to the bankruptcy trustee: cash, tax refunds, deposits (utility and rent), and all bank accounts are nonexempt. Because you are required to turn over only those nonexempt assets that you possess on the day and at the hour that the bankruptcy petition is filed with the court, many people try to protect assets by transferring ownership to someone else. However, there are strict rules regarding the transfer of assets just before filing bankruptcy, and you should know the law regarding transfers of any property. The federal exemptions (assets you can keep) include the following major items:

- Up to a $1,200 equity in your car.
- Up to a $7,500 equity in your home. This is commonly referred to as the *Homestead exemption.*
- Up to $200 in any particular item: household furnishings, appliances, clothing, books, animals, stereo, and any other electronic instruments.
- Up to $500 for all jewelry. In other words, you can keep one good watch.
- Books and tools used in your occupation, but your interest cannot exceed $750.
- Unmatured life insurance that you own. The law is complex on insurance, and you should check the code carefully as it applies to your particular situation.

- Any special medical equipment or aid that has been prescribed for you.
- Alimony or support as would be deemed reasonable.
- Social security benefits, unemployment compensation, veterans' benefits, public assistance benefits, and disability benefits.
- Payments, stock bonuses, pensions, profit sharing, annuities or similar benefit (but not IRAs) on account of illness, age, or disability—to the extent reasonably necessary for the support of the debtor and any dependents of the debtor.

There are technical exceptions regarding these exemptions, and if you are not sure about any benefits you are currently receiving, be sure to consult a competent attorney.

For an individual, a discharge in bankruptcy is an order issued by the court stating that the debtor's debts are forgiven. You do not have to pay any discharged debts. However, you may elect to pay your debts at a later time even though you are not obligated to do so under the bankruptcy law. Of course, many debts, such as taxes, alimony, and child support cannot be discharged. In a business Chapter 11 reorganization, business debts are reduced or otherwise modified and paid off over a period of time according to the reorganization plan. In a business liquidation (Chapter 7), debts are discharged, and there is no legal obligation to pay them. Only those debts that are included (listed) in a bankruptcy petition can be discharged.

A debtor can reaffirm a debt, meaning that a new agreement to repay a particular debt is entered into by the debtor with a creditor. As an example, if a debtor wishes to reaffirm the debt owed the holder of a mortgage on a home, the debtor must obtain court approval of the reaffirmation agreement if the agreement is to be enforceable. The agreement must be entered into before the granting of a discharge, and the court must find that the debt does not impose an undue hardship on the debtor and is in the debtor's best interest. Sometimes a reaffirmation agreement is entered into as a settlement of litigation regarding a possibly nondischargeable debt.

If you do not list a particular creditor, that debt will not be discharged. This is an important point. If you want to keep a particular credit source open, you should *exclude* that creditor from your petition. For example, you would not want to include the corner service station where your company's vehicles charge gas and repairs. Normally you want to keep such small accounts open so that you have access to basic necessities after filing bankruptcy. The same is true of an individual. If you want to continue using a particular charge card, pay it off on a monthly basis and do not list it in your petition. The law provides that the following debts cannot be discharged:

- Any debt resulting from fraud or misrepresentation by the debtor.
- Income and certain other taxes, as well as custom duties. For a business entity, all state and federal payroll taxes.
- A loan made on the basis of false information. As an example, if you gave your bank a false financial statement that induced it to extend or grant you a loan, that debt is not dischargeable.
- Any debts that were not listed in time for creditors to file a proof of claim.
- Debts for child support, alimony, or maintenance to a former spouse.
- Any penalties or fines owed to the government.
- Any debts owed to a governmental unit or a nonprofit organization for education (there are exceptions to this rule involving dates of loans and hardship factors).

Priority of Payments

The bankruptcy law provides for the following priority of payments:

1. Filing fees and administrative expenses related to the bankruptcy filing. This means the lawyers, accountants, the court, and creditors dealing with a debtor during the bankruptcy case get paid first.
2. Claims (unsecured) for wages, salaries, employee benefit plans, and commissions up to $2,000 per person, which must have been incurred within ninety days of the filing date of the bankruptcy or the closing of your business, whichever occurred first.

3. Deposits made by customers for purchase of goods or services (up to $900 each) before the bankruptcy filing that were not provided by your business.
4. Any unsecured claims by governmental units for income taxes, property, employment taxes, excise taxes, and custom duties.
5. Expenses incurred by the trustee in the sale and distribution of the funds to the creditors will also be paid from these funds.

A preference occurs when you arrange for a particular creditor to receive more than other creditors of the same category. Under the bankruptcy laws, you cannot make any preferential transfer for the benefit of a particular creditor within ninety days before filing your petition. All payments must be made in ordinary course of business, such as loan payments, utility bills, and any standard business bill that you would pay in the normal operation of your business.

There are different time restraints on different types of creditors. This aspect of the law applies to transfers of money or any other assets to insiders in your business or to outside friends or relatives. You should carefully check the specific code sections dealing with preferences before transferring any assets before a bankruptcy filing date. If any creditor does receive payments beyond her or his equitable share of a debtor's assets, the trustee can force the return of the excess portion. Payments made in the ordinary course of business (within forty-five days of payment) are not considered preferential transfers. Transfers to creditors from whom new value is obtained through new goods or services or new loans with new collateral provided are not considered preferences. The laws related to preference are a protection for both the debtor and the creditor because they ensure equal treatment under the law.

Creditors who have secured claims generally have priority over creditors with unsecured claims. For example, the claim of a creditor who has a certain piece of equipment as security for a loan has priority over that of a creditor who has simply extended trade credit to your business for monthly purchases of goods or services. A claim can have secured and unsecured parts, depending on the value of the property involved. If a property is worth less than the face amount of a claim, the claim is divided into an *allowed secured claim* (equal to the face value of the property) and an *allowed unsecured claim* equal to the dollar value of any deficiency. In a liquidation bankruptcy, secured creditors are often able to get their property returned to them before there is a final distribution to the unsecured creditors. Unsecured creditors have the next lowest priority in the distribution of funds after a liquidation. Equity owners such as partners or shareholders have the lowest priority.

Consequences of Filing Bankruptcy

In making your decision, you should be aware that a personal bankruptcy not only will ruin your credit rating for about ten years but will also seriously affect your reputation and credibility in looking for future work. Many employers now make a credit check part of the application process when you apply for a job.

A bankruptcy cannot be filed again for six years (once every six years). It may be difficult or impossible to obtain credit once a bankruptcy is filed because the filing becomes a public record, usually for a minimum of ten years. If you feel you will need a credit card after a bankruptcy, do not list the credit card as a debt to be discharged, and be sure to pay the balance in full before filing bankruptcy. It is even more difficult to obtain long-term loans, such as a home mortgage, after filing bankruptcy. It is possible to get the type of credit card that requires a savings account as collateral for the use of the card. When a Chapter 11 bankruptcy petition is filed, it may trigger state and local tax audits.

Checklist Points

1. Don't rush any decisions regarding bankruptcy. Take all the necessary time to make sure it is the only and the best solution in your circumstances.
2. Take advantage of the business resources you have. Ask your lawyer, accountant, and other professionals for advice and help in making your decision.
3. Before you take any final action, have your business assets appraised. Should you later file bankruptcy, a good appraisal will help you get more for your assets, and it may help you

convince creditors that they will benefit more from a reorganization than from a liquidation of your assets.

4. I recommend that you get the help of an experienced business bankruptcy lawyer before you make any final decisions.

5. An important consideration in deciding on the type of bankruptcy relief is the nature of the transactions between a corporation and its insiders (officers, directors, and shareholders). While an accountant will urge shareholders to take money rather than salary for repayment of loans to avoid personal income tax, bankruptcy analysis leads to the opposite conclusion because loan repayments are recoverable in a bankruptcy as preferences if made within one year prior to filing, while salaries are not preferential.

6. Filing bankruptcy may be very final, as in the case of a liquidation, or it may be the only way to save your company when all else has failed.

Epilogue: Now That You've Saved Your Business

If everyone sweeps before his own front door, then the street is clean.
—Goethe

Now that you've saved your business, what next? We are in a new business era that will focus on responsibility as opposed to irresponsibility for each other and for this world we all share. Disregard for the environment that sustains us all is no longer socially or morally acceptable. Instant worldwide communications and news reports quickly expose companies that use methods damaging to human and natural resources. And this exposure directly affects companies' bottom line: profits!

Your Employees

Values are changing rapidly, and employees are no longer satisfied with only monetary compensation. Individuals want to feel acknowledged as important and vital to a company. Thus environmental work needs to proceed from the inside out. This means taking a hard look at the internal environment in which your employees work. Happy employees miss less work, are more productive, and are a great source of word-of-mouth advertising in the community. This internal business environment includes the appearance of your physical plant, offices, warehouse, store, or other facility. Is it well maintained, clean, attractive, not cramped? Do you provide *space* for employees, such as a lunchroom or break room, and is it an attractive and comfortable place to be? Have you used color and interior design to create a pleasing atmosphere for your workers and customers as well? Drab and dreary colors or a lack of color is depressing for everyone. Do you have a way employees can easily communicate with each other? Many companies now have internal newsletters that employees can contribute to. There are many ways a business can contribute to the welfare of its employees, including:

- Flexible hours to accommodate employees' school or family obligations.
- Child care and elder care programs.
- Maternity leave, sick leave, and sabbaticals.
- Educational reimbursements.
- Company time for exercise programs or stress reduction programs.
- Birthday parties and birthday certificates or gifts.
- Company-sponsored picnics and outings.
- Regular company training sessions or seminars to keep employees up to date on progress and future plans. People like to be included.
- Work-at-home options where possible.
- Profit-sharing and retirement plans; medical and disability insurance.

Investments in human resources will pay off for a company in the long run. There is less turnover when workers are happy. People are more productive, harder working, and loyal when they see that a company values people and gives back to its employees more than just monetary compensation. Ultimately, job satisfaction is more important to most persons than money. How does a business improve job satisfaction? By improving the *quality* of life for its workers, and by providing challenging work for each individual, regardless of position or status.

Your Environment

Many companies are learning that it pays to be "green," or environmentally aware. More and more, consumers are basing buying decisions on a company's environmental policies. A 1989 Gallup poll revealed that 78 percent of Americans considered themselves environmentalists, and 40 percent said they would pay 10 percent more for a product that is considered environmentally safe.[1] As an example, companies that sell tuna have recently come under public scrutiny for fishing methods that kill thousands of dolphins and other sea creatures along with tuna. Many consumers now will not buy canned tuna from companies that continue such practices. Other companies lose business because customers reject their nonrecyclable packaging. Marketing studies continue to show that more and more customers are basing their buying decisions on whether a product is environmentally safe, and whether a company is environmentally responsible.

How does a business operate in a way that does not harm the environment or people? To start with, business decisions regarding manufacturing processes, product testing, design and packaging, advertising, and marketing should be based on a company philosophy that creates a needed product or service in such a way that the profits are never attained at the expense of others or of the environment. For example, a chemical plant may produce a valuable and needed product, but toxic by-products may be dumped into a stream or into the earth, endangering life. Lawsuits and other public reaction can put such a company out of business.

Is your packaging designed to minimize waste, and can it be recycled? Make sure that the top management knows what is going on at the bottom. The heads of a company should know all details of how a product is produced, from whom raw materials are obtained, and how are they obtained. In other words, responsibility should extend from beginning to end in order to ascertain a product's effect on both the environment and people. Are your business facilities designed to conserve energy and prevent unnecessary waste? Have you checked into recycling waste from your business?

The Body Shop is one of the largest natural cosmetic retailers in the world. A $300-million international company with over four hundred stores in thirty-four countries, the Body Shop sells only products that are all natural and "cruelty-free"—products that have not been tested on animals. The company has experienced tremendous consumer acceptance.[2] The company's stock has increased 600 percent in recent years. A company spokesperson stated that "it's investing in people." The Body Shop sponsors the International Boys Town Trust in southern India, several farm communities, and training programs for destitute boys. In addition, the Body Shop requires each employee to spend one hour each week in some type of community service; the employees are paid for this hour by the company.

I was just reading the label on a pint of Häagen-Dazs ice cream: "Dedicated to perfection" and "commitment to quality." I read on and discovered (by now the contents were half gone) that the company also buys most of its dairy cream and milk from small Vermont farms because it wants to support the small, independent family farm. This is a good example of a very successful company that has prospered because of a quality product, and because of its involvement in the community. Ben & Jerry's ice cream is another example of a company that stresses quality. It also donates some of its profits to preservation concerns and has created several ice cream products, including "Rainforest Crunch," made with ingredients from rain forest crops. Ben & Jerry's also practices some Japanese-style management methods, such as limiting top executives' pay to a maximum of ten times that of the lowest paid employee. Both companies' products cost more, but price doesn't seem to affect them at all. McDonald's recently reduced the thickness of its polystyrene containers and established a recycling program called "McRecycle." It is turning polystyrene waste into trays, high chairs and wastebaskets.

Many restaurants and other businesses now are paid for their empty glass and plastic containers. Instead of trash being an expense, it becomes an income-producing asset. Paper, plastics, glassware, metal containers and cans, tires, and numerous other waste or used products can now be recycled. Check your local area for recyclers.

Your Community

There are lots of ways businesses can help their community, by supporting local charities and youth groups, sponsoring little league teams, helping the elderly or homeless, and donating time, personnel, or funds to worthwhile community projects. It is a way to repay the community that provides most of the customers for a business in the first place. Take a good look at your immediate community. What are its needs that are not being taken care of? One company headquartered in a small town found out that the median strips on many of the city streets used to have shrubs and trees, but the city had let them deteriorate. Working with the city government, the company volunteered to help plant and care for new trees for the medians. You can imagine the reaction of people when they found out this company was helping to beautify their city. Where would you shop?

It is a natural human trait to give back to someone who gives; everyone benefits. You and I would like to buy our next car from the dealership that sponsored the local little league baseball team.

Your World

The public is demanding that business firms develop a social conscience, that they consider the social impact of their products or services in addition to economic considerations. In marketing and advertising, a business needs to reconsider how its advertising affects society as a whole. Whereas profits were once the number one consideration, now businesses must also weigh the social impact of their operations and the values society places on their activities.

Social marketing means that we must know the long-term effect of new products and technology. It is applying the principle of nonviolence in the business world. Regardless of how remarkable some new technology may be, it must be proved to be harmless both to individuals and to the world we live in. I am working on the manuscript for this book in front of a video monitor that, according to many studies, may be zapping me with radiation that could be affecting my health. We are all consumers and naively, perhaps, trust technology to help us improve the quality of our lives, but all too often, we suddenly find out that we are victims instead. The tremendous potential for new technologies to transform the quality of life for the better is threatened every time a business places profits ahead of human beings, as one auto company did when it decided that it was cheaper to settle lawsuits from exploding fuel tanks than to retool and move the gasoline tank, or to recall the defective autos already sold.

Growth just for growth's sake is no longer a viable option in the world we live in. Growth that naturally evolves out of a business enterprise's providing a needed, quality, harmless-to-life product or service is the only right growth. To borrow money in order to fuel growth out of greed and impatience for more or to accumulate companies simply wastes very precious resources.

True satisfaction in our working lives comes from doing something we love; then work is no longer work and becomes something unique that *only we* can do. This has nothing to do with size or quantity, but it has a lot to do with quality, simplicity, and creativity. A business that provides a worthwhile product or service in a way that adds to the quality of life is a worthwhile and invaluable enterprise. This is not to say that a large business is not beneficial, but the emphasis should be not on growth for growth's sake, but on the work itself.

Growth is a natural by-product of a successful business enterprise. We do our very best to provide a useful, worthwhile, quality product, and the growth takes care of itself, as does the money.

Growth for a business, or for an individual, must be tested in two ways: Will it add to the overall quality of life, and does it meet the test of harmlessness? Businesses need to develop a reciprocal, non-violent working relationship with this earth and the people who live on it—creating real value and quality in products and services. What we give of ourselves to others has a way of coming back to us multiplied many times over, often in surprising ways.

Appendix A:
Resources

Counseling and Professional Services

National Foundation for Consumer Credit
Primarily for individuals, there are 282 nonprofit counseling services that belong to the *National Foundation for Consumer Credit*. A directory can be obtained by writing to the NFCC at 8701 Georgia Ave., Suite 507, Silver Spring, MD 20910. Counselors will help you negotiate with your creditors. They can sometimes get better terms than you can. *Be careful* with commercial counselors. There are commercial counselors who do essentially what the nonprofit counselors do, but they charge fees (usually 15 percent) that are a percentage of your debt. There are many unscrupulous commercial counselors around who take your money and then ignore your problems. Check with your local Better Business Bureau before working with a commercial counselor.

U.S. Small Business Administration
Free management assistance publications and business development booklets are available from the U.S. Small Business Administration through local district offices of the SBA in the form of free management counseling and training from over eight thousand SCORE (Service Corps of Retired Executives) volunteers nationwide. The SBA has publications on financial management, business communications, business plans, choosing a retail location, strategic planning, productivity, marketing, crime prevention and small-business decision making. Some booklets are free. Others are priced from $.50 to $8.50. You can call your nearest SBA office, or write to 1725 I St., NW, Room 408, Washington, DC 20416. Phone: 800-368-5851 or 202-653-7561.

Small Business Development Centers
These centers are sponsored by the SBA and offer free counseling. To locate the center in your area, call 202-653-6768.

Government Publications

Small Business Reporter
Series by the Bank of America includes *Financial Records for Small Business, Avoiding Management Pitfalls,* and *Cash Flow/Cash Management.* Booklets cost $5.00. These can be ordered from Bank of America, Dept. 3120, Box 3700, San Francisco, CA 94317.

U.S. Department of Commerce
Publishes the *Directory of Federal and State Business Assistance: A Guide for New and Growing Companies.* It includes descriptions of over 182 federal and 500 state programs and services. Services offered include financial, marketing, information management, and networking. To obtain this publication, call or write the U.S. Department of Commerce—National Technical Information Service, 5825 Port Royal Rd., Springfield, VA 22101. Phone: 703-487-4650: Order number PB88-101977, price $29 plus $3 for postage and handling.

California Department of Commerce
The *Small Business Resource Directory,* published by the Small Business Development Center, is a directory of nonprofit small-business assistance organizations. These are organizations that provide a variety of services, including financial, marketing, management, and employee training help, to small business firms. Both public and private agencies are included. Contact the Small Business Development Center, 1121 L Street, Suite 600, Sacramento, CA 95814. Phone: 916-324-8102.

Self-Help Books

You will find some of these books in the self-help or business section of your local bookstore. If the book you want isn't on the shelf, you can ask the bookstore manager to order it for you, or you can order it directly from the publisher.

The One Minute Manager
By Kenneth Blanchard and Spencer Johnson (Berkley Books, New York, 1983). This book is an excellent, must-read book for every business owner, manager, or employee. It will help you manage yourself, your time, and others much more effectively with unusual and simple management techniques. Order from Berkley Publishing Group, 200 Madison Avenue, New York, NY 10016. Phone: 212-951-8800

The New Way to Compete
BY Harry A. Olson. This book explains innovative and new approaches to competition for anyone who must lead and motivate others.

Lexington Books, 866 Third Ave., New York, NY 10022. Phone: 800-323-7445.

Cash Flow Control Guide
By David H. Bangs, Upstart Publishing, $12.95 plus $3 shipping. Phone: 800-235-8866.

Integrated Direct Marketing: Techniques and Strategies for Success
By Ernan Roman (McGraw-Hill, New York, NY, 1988). This book gives clear guidelines on how to set up a marketing plan that's cost-effective and brings results.

The Essence of Leadership
By Edwin A. Locke. Locke presents a model for successful leadership that is based on real leaders, rather than abstract theory, distilling their characteristics into practical skills. Lexington Books, 866 Third Ave., New York, NY 10022. Phone: 800-323-7445.

The Small Business Bible
By Paul Resnik (John Wiley & Sons, New York, NY, 1988, $17.95). This book explains how to start a business and also how to manage growth.

Leading the Team Organization
By Dean W. Tjosvold and Mary M. Tjosvold. An excellent book for any reorganization effort. This is a valuable guide that will enable leaders and followers to empower each other to achieve common goals and create more profitable and successful organizations. Lexington Books, 866 Third Ave., New York, NY 10022. Phone: 800-323-7445.

The Addictive Organization
By Anne Wilson Schaef and Diane Fassel. This book deals with destructive behavior in business groups and in individuals who work in a business organization. The authors explore ways to change behavior and attitudes that perpetuate sick organizations. Harper & Row, Publishers, 10 East 53rd Street, New York, NY, 10022, 1988.

The Small Business Sourcebook
Published by Gale Research Company. Has sources of assistance and information related to 140 small business categories. Sources include associations, government agencies, franchising groups, reference works, consultants, and educational programs and institutions. Trade shows, start-up information, venture capital sources, and small-business development consultants are also included.

Gale's Encyclopedia of Business Information Services
(Sixth edition, 1986.) This book lists a wide variety of information sources in hundreds of different industries.

Financial Control for the Small Business
My Michael M. Coltman. How to maintain controls on profits and cash flow. Self-Counsel Press, Inc., 1303 North Northgate Way, Seattle, WA 98133. Phone: 604-986-3366.

A Tribute to Small Business: America's Growth Industry
Published by Pacific Bell, this booklet and a series of booklets, "Small Business Success" (1988) have articles on "Winning Ideas for Small Business Success" and "Young Entrepreneurs," plus a large directory of business resources. Pacific Bell also published "The Small Business Resource Guide," a listing of books, articles, governmental agencies, and other resources for a small business. Order from Pacific Bell Directory, Dept. CWS, One Rincon Center, 101 Spear St., Room 429, San Francisco, CA 94105.

Modern Inventory Operations
By Jan B. Young (Van Nostrand Reinhold, New York, NY, 1991). This book focuses on the types of inventory reports that are most useful, how to keep inventory records accurate, and how to understand and evaluate the newest warehouse technology—like having your own inventory consultant.

Annual Statement Studies
By Robert Morris Associates (1990, $95). This book will help you interpret financial statements and also compare your business financial statistics with those of other business firms in your same field. Available from RMA, 1 Liberty Place, Suite #2300, 1650 Market St., Philadelphia, PA 19103. Phone: 215-851-9100; fax 215-851-9206.

Almanac of Business and Industrial Financial Ratios
By Leo Troy (Prentice-Hall, Englewood Cliffs, NJ 07632, 1989, $49.95). Contains business data that help you determine the financial health of your business.

Bankruptcy: Do-It-Yourself
Explains exactly what bankruptcy is all about and how it affects your credit rating, property, and debts, with complete details on property you can keep under the state and federal exempt-property rules. Shows you step-by-step how to file bankruptcy by yourself. The book comes with all necessary forms and instructions. Order from Nolo Press, 950 Parker St., Berkeley, CA 94710 ($14.95).

Chapter 13: The Federal Plan to Repay Your Debts
This book explains how an individual develops a plan to pay most of
his or her debts over a three-year period. Chapter 13 is an alternative
to straight bankruptcy, and it ends creditor harassment, wage attach-
ments, and other collection efforts. This book contains all necessary
forms and worksheets. Order from Nolo Press, 950 Parker St., Berkeley, CA 94710 ($12.95).

How to Get Out of Debt and Stay Out of Debt
By Merle E. Dowd. This is a very helpful book which gives individuals
a systematic method of reorganizing their financial affairs and getting
out of debt, with special emphasis on personal budgeting and planning.
Order from Henry Regnery Company, 114 West Illinois St., Chicago,
IL 60610.

Business Law
By N. T. Henley. A comprehensive book on all aspects of business law
including torts and crimes, partnerships, corporations, landlord and tenant contracts, commercial transactions, and bankruptcy law. Order from
Holt, Rinehart Publishing, 383 Madison Ave., New York, NY 10017.

Collier Bankruptcy Practice Guide
This is an authoritative legal guide to bankruptcy, which is updated
annually. It is published by Matthew Bender & Co., 11 Penn Plaza,
New York, NY 10001.

Trade Associations

Bartering   International Reciprocal Trade Association, Great Falls,
VA. 9513 Beach Mill Rd., Great Falls, VA 22066. Write for information packet.

National Association of Trade Exchanges
Euclid, Ohio. Phone: 800-733-6283. 10556 Riverside Drive, Toluca
Lake, CA 91602.

Advertising and Marketing Aids

That's Our New Ad Campaign
By Dick Wasserman. How to create better ads. An excellent guide for
CEOs, presidents, ad managers, account executives, art directors, copy-
writers, and students. Lexington Books, 866 Third Ave., New York, NY
10022. 800-323-7445.

How to Write a Good Advertisement
By Victor Schwab. A commonsense guide on every aspect of copywriting, includes 100 good headlines and why they were profitable, what the illustration should and should not do, 22 ways to hold the reader's attention, and many others. Harper & Row, Publishers, Inc., 10 East 53rd St., New York, NY 10022.

Direct Mail Copy That Sells!
By Herschell Lewis. An excellent book on how to write advertising copy. Includes the four great motivators, simple word changes that can double the impact of your ads, and how to write catalog copy. Order from Prentice-Hall, Inc., Englewood Cliffs, NJ.

Successful Direct Marketing Methods
By Bob Stone. One of the best textbooks on direct marketing around. Includes media selection, creating effective ads, mathematics of direct marketing, creating catalogs, and testing techniques. Order from Crain Books, 740 Rush St., Chicago, Ill 60611.

Graphics Today
A magazine with articles geared to visual communications, designing brochures, reports, booklets, and other advertising-related publications. Write Syndicate Magazines, 6 East 43rd St., New York, NY 10017.

Business Ethics and Philosophy

Critical Path
By R. Buckminster Fuller. *Critical Path* traces the origins and evolution of humanity's social, political, and economic systems from prehistory, through the development of the great political empires, to the vast international corporate and political systems that control our destiny today. An eye-opening book that digs out the truth about what has happened economically to all of us. St. Martin's Press, 175 Fifth Ave., New York, NY 10010 (1981).

Up Against the Corporate Wall
By S. Prakash Sethi. Examines modern corporations and the ethical and social issues they face. Contains real-world case studies of the issues confronting a modern business. Prentice-Hall, Inc., Englewood Cliffs, NJ 07632, 201-592-2000; Route 9 West, Englewood Cliffs, NJ 07632.

State of the World
By Lester R. Brown. Examines our relationship with the earth and its natural system and how the scale of human activities is affecting the

world. Explores economics and environmental issues. Penguin Books Canada Ltd., 2801 John St., Markham, Ontario L3R 1B4.

Legal Reference

National Association for Independent Paralegals
This association can put you in touch with a paralegal who can help you with many legal procedures, especially filing forms and other paperwork. A paralegal is a much lower priced alternative than traditional lawyers. Phone: 800-542-0034.

Debtor-Creditor Law in a Nut Shell
A comprehensive reference book for legal problems arising from debtor–creditor relations. Topics include debt collection, rights of creditors, collective creditor actions, bankruptcy overview, pre- and post-bankruptcy transfers, bankruptcy and secured claims, Chapter 7 bankruptcy, leases and contracts, discharge in bankruptcy, and Chapter 11 bankruptcy. Order from West Publishing Company, P.O. Box 64526, St. Paul, MN 55164-0526.

Everybody's Guide to Small Claims Court
By Ralph Warner. How to collect bills more effectively. Nolo Press, 950 Parker St., Berkeley, CA 94710.

Business Agreements: A Complete Guide to Oral and Written Contracts
How to understand contracts and how to write, read, and interpret contracts. A Chilton Guide; available in bookstores or libraries.

The Directory of Bankruptcy Attorneys
Prentice-Hall Law and Business, 1989, $140. To order, call 201-894-8484. Your local library may have a copy of this book.

One Step Ahead: The Legal Aspects of Business Growth
By Andrew Sherman. Amacom Books, 135 W. 50th, New York, NY 10020; 1989, $22.95. Phone: 212-903-8081.

Legal Forms

Legal Forms for Smaller Businesses
An excellent assortment of over 200 legal forms and agreements you can use for almost any legal purpose. Forms include credit and collections, leases and tenancies, loans and borrowing, employment, and debt extension. All forms are perforated and ready for use ($21.95). Order

from J. K. Lasser Tax Institute, c/o Simon & Schuster, 200 Old Tappan Rd., Old Tappan, NJ 07675.

Wolcotts Legal Forms and Stationery
This company carries over five hundred legal forms for all purposes. Most stationery stores have their catalog or a similar one. 214 S. Spring St., Los Angeles, CA 90012. Phone: 213-624-4943.

Business Services

Dun & Bradstreet
D&B provides a variety of services for the business owner, including collection and credit-rating services. Write for their free brochure: Dun & Bradstreet Commercial Collection Division, 225 Broadway, New York, NY 10007.

The American Woman's Economic Development Corporation
A nonprofit corporation formed to assist women in business. Services include a telephone hot line, counseling, and other low-cost programs. For information, write 60 E. 42nd St., New York, NY 10165.

The National Association for the Self-Employed
Discounted legal and accounting services, toll-free telephone lines, a newsletter, and other business services are offered, plus group health insurance plans. Write for information: 2324 Gravel Rd., Fort Worth, TX 76118.

The Small Business Service Bureau
A national organization for small business owners that provides information, management advice, and legislative advocacy for its members. Write 544 Main St., Worcester, MA 01601.

Paychex Payroll Service
An excellent company that can handle all your payroll needs economically and efficiently. It files all required tax reports and can pay taxes electronically for you. It maintains offices in all major U.S. cities. Paychex corporate headquarters: 911 Panorama Trail South, P.O. Box 25397, Rochester, NY 14625-9986.

Safe Banks
A computer study published by Command Productions, a banking research firm, lists two thousand, twenty-four hundred banks it has rated "safe" on the basis of Federal Reserve data. For $29, they will send you a custom report on your bank and the latest update of the safe list. P.O. Box 2223, San Francisco, CA 94126. Phone: 415-332-3161.

Bank Rating Reports
Published by Veribank, Inc. This company compiles computer analyses of more than thirty thousand federally insured financial institutions, using figures released by regulatory agencies. For $20, they will send you a report that rates your bank, savings-and-loan, or credit union. P.O. Box 2963, Woburn, MA 01888. Phone: 617-245-8370.

The National Association of Temporary Services
Contact this association to find out which temporary help companies serve your area or to request a free directory. Alexandria, VA. Phone: 703-549-6287.

Appendix B:
Forms You Can Copy*

Creditor Repayment Plan
Monthly Cash Flow Analysis
Revised Monthly Cash Flow Analysis
Cash Flow Projection
Cash Flow Variance Report

The following forms provided courtesy of J. K. Lasser Tax Institute, 200 Old Tappan Road, Old Tappan, New Jersey 07675:

Agreement to Compromise Debt
Agreement to Extend Debt Payment
Extension of Agreement
Installment Promissory Note
Amendment to Lease
Sublease

* Neither the author nor the publisher is engaged in rendering legal advice. If legal advice is required, the services of an attorney should be obtained. The publisher and the author assume no responsibility regarding the proper use of any legal forms contained in this book.

CREDITOR REPAYMENT PLAN

CREDITOR NAME	TOTAL OWED	AMOUNT PAST DUE	DAYS PAST DUE	NEW MONTHLY PAYMENT	NO. OF PMTS	CASH FLOW CREATED
TOTALS:						

Monthly Cash Flow Analysis		
CASH RECEIPTS (Expected from Accounts Receivable)		$
CASH RECEIPTS (From Cash Sales)		
TOTAL CASH AVAILABLE		$
MONTHLY EXPENSES:		
Purchases for Resale	$	
Rent: Building & Equipment		
Salaries		
Executive Salaries		
Payroll Taxes		
Fringe Benefits		
Accounting & Legal		
Advertising		
Office Supplies & Postage		
Insurance		
Utilities		
Operating Supplies		
Telephone		
Auto Expense		
Miscellaneous		
Bank Loan (Principal)		
Bank Loan (Interest)		
Other Loans		
TOTAL MONTHLY EXPENSE		$
CASH FLOW FOR MONTH		$

Revised Monthly Cash Flow Analysis		
BEGINNING CASH		$
CASH RECEIPTS		
TOTAL CASH AVAILABLE		$
MONTHLY EXPENSES:		
Payments to Vendors (Repayment Plan)	$	
Purchases: Current Month (Cash or on account)		
Rent: Building & Equipment		
Salaries		
Executive Salaries		
Payroll Taxes		
Fringe Benefits		
Accounting & Legal		
Advertising		
Office Supplies & Postage		
Insurance		
Utilities		
Operating Supplies		
Telephone		
Auto Expense		
Miscellaneous		
Bank Loan (Principal)		
Bank Loan (Interest)		
Other Loans		
TOTAL MONTHLY EXPENSE		$
CASH FLOW FOR MONTH		$

Cash Flow Projection	Period:		
	MONTH-1	MONTH-2	MONTH-3
BEGINNING CASH	$	$	$
CASH RECEIPTS			
TOTAL CASH AVAILABLE	$	$	$
EXPENSES:			
Payments to Vendors (Repayment Plan)	$	$	$
Purchases: Current Month (Cash or on account)			
Rent: Building & Equipment			
Salaries			
Executive Salaries			
Payroll Taxes			
Fringe Benefits			
Accounting & Legal			
Advertising			
Office Supplies & Postage			
Insurance			
Utilities			
Operating Supplies			
Telephone			
Auto Expense			
Miscellaneous			
Bank Loan (Principal)			
Bank Loan (Interest)			
Other Loans			
TOTAL CASH PAID OUT	$	$	$
ENDING CASH	$	$	$

Cash Flow Variance Report	For Month of:		
	Budget	Actual	Variance
BEGINNING CASH	$	$	$
CASH RECEIPTS			
TOTAL CASH AVAILABLE	$	$	$
EXPENSES:			
Payments to Vendors (Repayment Plan)	$	$	$
Purchases: Current Month (Cash or on Account)			
Rent: Building & Equipment			
Salaries			
Executive Salaries			
Payroll Taxes			
Fringe Benefits			
Accounting & Legal			
Advertising			
Office Supplies & Postage			
Insurance			
Utilities			
Operating Supplies			
Telephone			
Auto Expense			
Miscellaneous			
Bank Loan (Principal)			
Bank Loan (Interest)			
Other Loans			
TOTAL CASH PAID OUT	$	$	$
ENDING CASH	$	$	$

Agreement to Compromise Debt

FOR GOOD CONSIDERATION, the undersigned as a creditor of _____ (Debtor) hereby enters into this agreement to compromise the indebtedness due the undersigned on the following terms and conditions:

1. The Debtor and the undersigned acknowledge that the present debt due and owing is in the amount of $

2. The parties agree that the undersigned shall accept the sum of $ as full and total payment on said debt and in complete discharge and settlement of all monies presently due, provided the sum herein shall be fully and punctually paid in the manner following:

3. In the event the Debtor fails to fully and punctually pay the compromised amount, the undersigned creditor shall have full rights to prosecute the claim for the original debt due less payments made.

4. In the event of default in payment the Debtor agrees to pay all reasonable attorneys' fees and costs of collection.

5. This agreement shall be binding upon and inure to the benefit of the parties, their successors, assigns and personal representatives.

Signed under seal this   day of   , 19   .

In the presence of: _____
                           Creditor

_____   _____
                           Debtor

Reprinted with permission of J. R. Lasser Tax Institute.

Agreement to Extend Debt Payment

FOR VALUE RECEIVED, the undersigned
                    (Creditor) and   (Debtor)
hereby acknowledge and agree that:

1. The Debtor presently owes the Creditor the sum of $,
   said sum being presently due and payable, but that
   Debtor is unable to fully pay same at present.
2. In further consideration of the Creditor's forebearance, the
   Debtor agrees to pay said debt on extended terms in the
   manner following:
3. In the event the Debtor fails to make any payments punctually on the agreed extended terms, the Creditor shall
   have full rights to proceed for the collection of the entire
   balance then remaining.
4. In the event of default in payment the Debtor agrees to
   pay all reasonable attorneys' fees and costs of collection.
5. This agreement shall be binding upon and inure to the
   benefit of the parties, their successors, assigns and personal representatives.

   Signed under seal this   day of   , 19   .

   _____
   Creditor

   _____
   Debtor

Reprinted with permission of J. R. Lasser Tax Institute.

Extension of Agreement

Extension of Agreement made by and between
(First Party), and
(Second Party), said agreement being dated
, 19 (Agreement).

Whereas said Agreement expires on , 19 ,
and the parties desire to extend and continue said Agree-
-ment, it is provided that said Agreement shall be extended
for an additional term commercing upon the expiration of the
original term and expiring on , 19 .

This extension shall be on the same terms and conditions as contained in the original Agreement and as set forth
and incorporated herein excepting that: (Describe any new or
changed terms.)

This extension of Agreement shall be binding upon and inure
to the benefit of the parties, their successors and assigns.

Signed under seal this day of , 19 .
In the presence of:

_____ _____

_____

Reprinted with permission of J. R. Lasser Tax Institute.

Installment Promissory Note

FOR VALUE RECEIVED, the undersigned jointly and severally promise to pay to the order of
the sum of ($) Dollars, together with interest thereon at the rate of % per annum on any unpaid balance.

Said sum, inclusive of interest, shall be paid in installments of $ each, with a first payment due , 19 , and the same amount on the same day of each (month/week) thereafter until the full principal amount of this note and accrued interest is fully paid. All payments shall be first applied to earned interest and the balance to principal. The undersigned may pre-pay this note in whole or in part without penalty.

This note shall be fully payable upon demand of any holder in the event the undersigned shall default in making any payments due under this note within days of its due date.

In the event of any default, the undersigned agree to pay all reasonable attorneys' fees and costs of collection to the extent permitted by law. This note shall take effect as a sealed instrument and be enforced in accordance with the laws of the payee's state. All parties to this note waive presentment, demand, protest, and all notices thereto, and agree to remain fully bound notwithstanding any extension, indulgence, modification or release or discharge of any party or collateral under this note.

Signed under seal this day of , 19 .
In the presence of:

_____   _____

_____   _____

Amendment to Lease

FOR GOOD CONSIDERATION,
(Landlord), and   (Tenant), under a
certain lease agreement between them for premises known as
                             , dated   , 19   , hereby
modify and amend said Lease in the following particulars:
(Described modified terms)

   This lease amendment shall be binding upon and inure to
the benefit of the parties, their successors, assigns and personal representatives.
   All other Lease terms shall remain as contained in the original Lease.

   Signed under seal this   day of   , 19   .

_____
Landlord

_____
Tenant

Reprinted with permission of J. R. Lasser Tax Institute.

Sublease

1. Parties: This sublease was entered into between
      (Tenant) and   (Subtenant).
2. Sublease Period: The Subtenant agrees to lease
                          (Described property to be leased)
from

                              to
3. Terms of Sublease: The Subtenant agrees to comply with
   all terms and conditions of the lease entered into by the
   Tenant, including the prompt payment of all rents. The
   lease agreement is incorporated into this agreement by
   reference. The Subtenant agrees to pay the Landlord the
   monthly rent stated in that lease, which is $.
4. Security Deposit: The Subtenant agrees to pay to Tenant
   the sum of $ as a security deposit.
5. Consideration: The Subtenant agrees to pay the Tenant the
   sum of $ in consideration of this agreement.
6. Inventory: Attached to this agreement is an inventory of
   items or fixtures that were in the above-described property on   , 19   . The Subtenant agrees to replace
   or reimburse the Tenant for any of these items that are
   missing or damaged.
7. Landlord's Consent: The Landlord consents to this sublease
   and agrees to promptly notify the Tenant at
                  if the Subtenant is in breach of this
   agreement. Nothing herein shall constitute a release of
   Tenant, who shall remain bound under this lease.

_____   _____
Landlord   Date   Tenant   Date

                                 _____
                                 Subtenant   Date

Reprinted with permission of J. R. Lasser Tax Institute.

Glossary of Legal and Business Terms

ABC Analysis A method used to control inventory investment. "A" items account for 50 percent of your total sales; "B" items, 25 percent; and "C" items, the next 20 percent. The remaining 5 percent are not considered significant. The dollar amount of inventory is then calculated for each category, the intent being to reduce excess inventory in the slower selling B and C categories.

Acceleration Clause A clause that permits the full amount of a debt to become due upon the occurrence of some event, such as not paying an installment on time.

Acceptance Under contract law, acceptance means the agreement to the proposed terms of a contract by the party receiving the proposal.

Accord and Satisfaction An *accord* occurs when one party to a contract or obligation agrees to accept something less than or different from an existing obligation or agreement. In this process the original obligation is null and void. *Satisfaction* refers to the other party's acceptance of the considerations offered. Their satisfaction or acceptance is the action that extinguishes the old contract or obligation. However, it should be noted that the old obligation is not voided until the new terms of the agreement are fully performed.

Accounting Equation Usually stated as: Assets = Liabilities + Owner's Equity

Account Receivable A record of money owed that is unpaid.

Accounts Payable Money you owe to your suppliers for items you have purchased from them. Usual payment terms are thirty days from the billing date, although in different industries payment terms may be for longer or shorter periods.

Accounts Receivable Aging   The process of determining how long your customers have owed you money, commonly broken down into thirty, sixty, and ninety days and over.

Account Stated   An agreement between a creditor and a debtor that states that all amounts owed are correct and are due. An account stated becomes a binding contract when both creditor and debtor agree to the amounts involved.

Adjudication   The legal process by which a dispute is resolved.

Adjustment Case   A Chapter 13 bankruptcy procedure that allows a person to pay his or her debts over an extended period of time, usually three years, from future wages or salary.

Adverse Possession   Adverse possession is the acquiring of actual title to real property by taking possession of the property without the owner's consent and continuing possession publicly for a period of time set by law.

Agency   The relationship created by a contract, agreement, or law between a principal and an agent, where the actions of the agent are binding on the principal.

Aging Schedule   A report that shows how long accounts receivable have been outstanding. It gives the dollar amounts outstanding by periods: current, 30 days, 60 days, 90 days and so on.

Agreement   A meeting of the minds between two or more parties, which may or may not be a contract.

Alteration (Material)   The modification of the terms of an agreement or contract that results in material changes in the agreement.

Amendment   The alteration of a right, law, or interest, which often is binding when a certain required action is completed.

Amortization   Certain business expenses can be written off over an extended period of time, such as the cost of forming a business, of a restaurant liquor license, or of a patent.

Annual Percentage Rate   The total of all items that make up a finance charge or interest charges expressed as an annual percentage rate.

Answer   A defendant's response to a complaint or petition.

Anticipatory Breach   Occurs when a contract is broken before the time of performance has occurred. It allows the nonbreaching party to the contract to seek a legal remedy.

Apparent Authority   Authority implied by the words or conduct of a principal that causes a third person to believe the agent has the authority.

Apparent Intent   The motive of a person as indicated by her or his words or actions when interpreted by a reasonable person.

Arbitration   Submitting a dispute to a third party for settlement.

Asset-Based Lender   A lender that bases its loan on the specific value of tangible assets, such as a vehicle, a printing press, a computer system, accounts receivable, or inventory. The financial strength of the business is not of primary importance to this type of lender.

Assignee   One to whom an assignment is made.

Assignment   The transfer of certain rights or interests to a third person, who cannot receive any greater rights than the transferor. Example: Many leases have clauses *prohibiting* assignment without consent of the landlord.

Assignment for the Benefit of Creditors   A debtor voluntarily transfers her or his property to a trustee or other third party, who then liquidates the assets and pays the creditors out of the proceeds. This is a business liquidation process and is entered into when you have decided to liquidate your business affairs. However, this is a nonbankruptcy form of liquidation.

Assignor   The person who makes an assignment.

Attachment   A legal proceeding that permits a plaintiff to have nonexempt property of the defendant seized and a lien placed on the property as security. Example: The Doe Co. has $5,000 in lawnmowers in a warehouse. Doe Co. owes Happy Creditor, Inc., $10,000. Happy Creditor, Inc., can apply to the court for an *attachment lien* to freeze the $5,000 worth of lawnmowers until its lawsuit against Doe Co. is completed.

Attestation   Witnessing a document and signing as a witness.

Automatic Stay   A court order that, once a bankruptcy petition is filed, automatically halts legal actions such as wage garnishments, collections or lawsuits, and foreclosures. This also prohibits a state from beginning or continuing any attempt to revoke a debtor's business license for nonpayment of taxes. However, an automatic stay cannot prevent tax audits.

Average Age of Receivables   Trade account receivables divided by the year's sales multiplied by 365. The average length of time a business waits after making a sale before receiving payment.

Avoidable Cost   Costs that will not be incurred when a business operation or segment is discontinued.

Balance Sheet   A financial report showing the financial position of a company on a specific date in terms of assets, liabilities, and owner's equity.

Bankruptcy   A legal procedure under the Federal Bankruptcy Law enabling a business or individual who is unable to pay his or her debts to be declared insolvent, or bankrupt. Assets (nonexempt) are distributed to creditors, and the debt is released from all further payment on most debts.

Bankruptcy Reform Act of 1978   An entirely new Bankruptcy Act enacted to facilitate debtor reorganizations.

Bilateral Contract   A contract formed by a mutual exchange of promises.

Bill of Lading   A document of title that is evidence of the receipt of goods for shipment, with instructions for shipping to the carrier. A bill of lading can be either negotiable or nonnegotiable. When it is negotiable, it is both a receipt and evidence of title (ownership) of the shipped goods.

Breach of Duty   The failure to fulfill a legal promise or obligation.

Break-Even Point   The level of business volume at which total costs are equal to total revenues. A break-even analysis determines what level of sales are required to meet a business firm's basic expenses. Profits do not begin to accrue until sales volume exceeds the break-even point.

Bulk Transfer   A transfer of materials, inventory, merchandise, equipment, or supplies in quantities or under circumstances that cause the transfer to be not in the ordinary course of the transferor's business.

Business Judgment Rule   A rule that protects corporate managers from responsibility for honest errors of judgment.

Business Trust   A legal arrangement in which the ownership and management of property is transferred to trustees, who are given the authority to operate the business for the original owners.

Cancellation   Generally the termination or revoking or destruction of a contract. As an example, if the parties to a contract both agree to tear up a contract, it is canceled. There are other ways in which a contract may be canceled, through a breach of the terms by one of the parties, and so on.

Capacity   The legal ability to perform an act, as in the creating of a contract or other legal agreement.

Cash Flow   The supply, or flow, of cash through a business after all cash outflows are subtracted. A business can have a negative or positive cash flow.

Chapter 7   Also called a *straight bankruptcy.* Used by debtors to wipe out their unsecured debts. This type of bankruptcy is either for an individual or for a business in which assets are liquidated by a court-appointed trustee except for those particular assets that are exempt under the bankruptcy statutes.

Chapter 11 Reorganization   A legal procedure under the Federal Bankruptcy Code that permits a debtor to remain in business free from harassment by creditors or lenders, while a specific reorganization plan is put together to pay creditors and also rehabilitate the business under the protection of the bankruptcy court. While used primarily by corporations and partnerships, Chapter 11 may also be used by an individual.

Chapter 13   A legal process in which a salaried *individual* (not a business or its owner/investor) debtor is protected from creditors' collection efforts while keeping all of his or her property and attempting to pay off all or part of his or her debts within a three-year period. It is a personal financial reorganization.

Charging Order   A legal action requiring that a partner's share of partnership profits be paid directly to a creditor until the debt is paid.

Chattel   Any tangible property or interest in a tangible property other than real property.

Chattel Mortgage   The conditional transfer of a legal interest in personal property as security for a debt or other obligation. This is commonly called a *security interest.*

Chattel Paper   Any document that is evidence of both a monetary obligation and a security interest.

Collateral   Property that is subject to a security interest in a secured transaction.

Collateral Note   A note that has personal property as security.

Combination Agreement   An agreement that combines the features of composition and extension agreements. Creditors' claims are reduced by a set percentage agreed upon by all creditors. In this case, part of the debt is paid over an extended period of time, with an initial cash payment at the time of finalizing the agreement.

Commercial Contract   A commercial (business) contract between two or more individuals. An example is an agreement to purchase a stipulated amount of a particular product from a specific supplier.

Commercial Impracticability   A legal principle that excuses a seller from delivering a product or performing a service because of an unforeseen event(s) that results in performance becoming extraordinarily difficult.

Commercial Paper   Written promises or obligations to pay amounts of money. The term applies to both negotiable and nonnegotiable instruments.

Community Property   Property that is co-owned by a husband and a wife, usually including all that is owned or acquired after marriage (except by gift or inheritance), regardless of who acquired it.

Compensatory Damages   A sum of money awarded by a court for actual losses sustained because of a wrong committed by another individual.

Complaint   The document filed in court by the plaintiff, often called a *petition,* explaining the plaintiff's cause of action.

Composition of Creditors   An agreement (also known as a *composition agreement* or a *compromise agreement*) between a debtor and his or her creditors that each creditor will accept a lesser amount than the debt owed as full satisfaction of that debt. This type of agreement is an alternative to bankruptcy. The lesser amount paid is an agreed-upon percentage and is the same for all creditors who participate in the agreement. The payments are usually paid as one cash payment at the time the agreements are finalized. The purpose of a composition agreement is to enable a business to recover financially. A composition agreement is more common for more serious business difficulties in which other, more simple agreements, such as an extension agreement, will not work. A composition agreement can work well for a firm that has suffered permanent losses to assets because of events outside the firm's control, such as natural disasters or riots.

Compromise Agreement   The result of a process often called a *compromise and settlement.* It is an agreement that may be entered into with one or a group of creditors, not necessarily all of one's creditors. A compromise agreement is legally binding on all parties to the agreement, and it also forbids reopening old issues related to the original controversy.

Condition A clause in a contract that, on the occurrence or nonoccurrence of a certain event, creates or terminates the duties of both parties to the contract.

Conditional Endorsement Occurs when an endorser agrees to be liable in a contract or agreement only if a specific event happens.

Conditional Sales Contract A contract for the sale of goods in which the seller retains title until the goods are paid for in full by the buyer. This contract is in force even though the buyer may have physical possession of the goods. A conditional sale contract is sometimes referred to as a *security interest*.

Condition Concurrent A specific clause in a contract stipulating that both parties' performances are to occur simultaneously.

Condition Precedent A specific condition that must first take place before either party is bound by the contract.

Confession of Judgment An agreement that allows a creditor to get a court judgment without the usual legal proceedings if a debt is not paid according to the agreed-upon terms. Thus a creditor can bypass the usual court procedures involved with collecting a debt.

Consideration An inducement offered and accepted in the process of forming a contract—something done or given or to be given in exchange for a promise—the most common consideration being a sum of money.

Contract An agreement between two or more persons that establishes a legal relationship and that is legally enforceable provided there is sufficient consideration.

Contribution Margin The excess of revenue over variable costs, or the amount contributed toward the absorption of fixed costs and the generation of profits.

Conversion Any action in which personal property of another is wrongfully appropriated for one's own use, or in which one unlawfully interferes with a person's right to use and enjoy her or his property.

Conveyance Transferring or conveying an interest in or title to a property to another.

Corporate Opportunity A legal principle preventing corporate officers, directors, or corporate managers from *personally* benefiting from business circumstances that should benefit the corporation. Example: A manager has been authorized to purchase land or property for the corporation and receives from the seller of the property a kickback that is deposited in the manager's personal account.

Corporate Stock   Shares of stock issued by a corporation in order to raise capital. Each share represents an ownership interest in the business.

Cosigner   An individual who guarantees the repayment of a debt. Although the debtor's obligation to pay the debt can be discharged in a bankruptcy proceeding, the cosigner is still liable for the debt unless the cosigner also declares bankruptcy. Example: Creditors of small companies often require the real owner to cosign personally in order to guarantee repayment of a debt of the company.

Cost Behavior Analysis   A study of how specific costs react to changes in sales volume.

Counteroffer   A new offer made in response to an offer, with different terms from the original offer. A proposal of this type is commonly taken to be a rejection of the original offer.

Course of Dealing   Past conduct or actions between two parties becomes the basis for interpreting their present conduct or agreement regarding the terms of a contract.

Course of Performance   A contract for the sale of goods involves many occasions for performance, which are known by both parties and not objected to by either; this repeated performance becomes the basis for interpreting the remaining contract terms.

Creditor   A person, business, or government agency to whom money is owed.

Creditor's Agreement   A contract with a business firm's creditors that stipulates the resolution of outstanding debts in a nonbankruptcy format. This type of agreement is sometimes referred to as a *workout agreement,* an *out-of-court agreement,* or a *rehabilitation plan.* This type of an agreement may provide for payment in full of a debt over an extended period of time (*extension agreement*), or the payment may be an amount agreed upon that is less than the actual amount of the debt (*composition agreement*).

Creditors' Committee   A committee made up of a debtor's creditors, which manages the debtor's financial affairs until his or her debts are paid off. The committee is formed by mutual agreement of the debtor and creditors and is commonly part of the debtor's payment plan.

Current Ratio   Often referred to by bankers as the *acid test,* this ratio is obtained by dividing current assets by current liabilities.

Damages   Reparation in money recovered by a person who has suffered losses as a result of the unlawful acts or negligence of another.

Debit   A debt charged to an account; for example, a debit charge reduces a bank account.

Debt   A legal obligation to pay money.

Debt Ratio   Total debt divided by total assets.

Debtor   The individual, business, or other entity who owes money.

Debt Securities   Instruments representing corporate debt that can be secured either by specific corporate assets or by a general corporate obligation to pay the debt.

De Facto Merger   An informal type of merger that is formed by acquiring stock or other assets.

Default   Failure or neglect to fulfill a legal obligation or requirement, as in the failure to pay a debt when due.

Defendant   The party (may be an individual or a business) defending or denying a claim of the plaintiff.

Deficiency Judgment   A judgment against a debtor in which the value of the collateral for the debt is less than the amount owed. Example: The bank repossesses your car and sells it at auction, but the sale price is less than the amount you owe on the car. The court can issue a *deficiency judgment* for the difference, which you will have to pay.

Delegation   The transferring of the right to represent or act for another. It is commonly called the *delegation of duties to a third party.*

Demand Instrument   An instrument that is payable on demand when the holder presents it. Example: You have signed a note for $5,000 payable on demand. The next day, the lender decides he would like his money back. He presents the note and demands immediate payment, and you have to return the $5,000.

Depository Bank   The first bank where an instrument is sent for collection.

Destination Contract   A contract that requires the seller to offer goods to a buyer at a specific place stipulated by the buyer.

Disaffirmance   The setting aside or legal avoidance of an obligation. An example is the almost universal rule that all contracts with minors are voidable. This rule protects younger persons from being taken advantage of by unethical business practices. In most states, eighteen is the legal age of consent. Not all contracts can be disaffirmed solely on the basis of age; the most notable exceptions are marriage and contracts to enlist in the armed forces.

Dischargeable Debt   A debt that can be legally forgiven by the bankruptcy court.

Discharge in Bankruptcy   The legal forgiveness of a debt issued by the bankruptcy court, usually several months after bankruptcy is filed. The release frees the person from any further liability on dischargeable debts filed during the proceedings.

Disclaimer   A stipulation in a sales or other contract that tries to prevent creation of a warranty. Example: An accountant informs the readers of a financial statement that an audit has not been completed and therefore the accuracy of the statements cannot be guaranteed.

Dissolution   The breaking up or termination of a corporation or partnership.

Earnest Money   A deposit paid to a seller of goods or services that holds the seller to a contractual obligation. Often this sum of money becomes liquidated damages if the buyer defaults on the contract.

Economic Duress   The unlawful use of threats, economic pressure, or other actions intended to overcome an individual's use of free will and that induces the person to do something that he or she would not otherwise do.

Endorsement   The signature of one signing a contract, agreement, or other instrument with the purpose of transferring the instrument and also setting the limits of liability.

Equity   The value of property after the deduction of any debts owed on the property.

Equity Kicker   Also referred to as a *participation loan*. This type of loan is most commonly seen in business start-ups. The lender receives a part ownership in the business in addition to principle and interest payments.

Equity Securities   Shares of capital stock in a corporation that represent an ownership interest.

Escrow Agent   An agent who holds assets of one party with the authority to transfer the assets to a specified person when a particular event happens.

ESOP   Employee stock ownership plan. Employees purchase part of a business.

Exculpatory Clause   A clause in a contract in which one party agrees to free the other party of all liability in the event that he or she suffers monetary or physical damages.

Executed Contract   A contract that has been completely performed by both parties to the contract.

Executory Contract   A contract that is unperformed by at least one of the parties involved.

Exempt Property   Property that a debtor is allowed to keep after a bankruptcy. Exempt property cannot be seized to satisfy a debt.

Express Authority   The specific authority given to an agent by the principal.

Express Contract   A contract that is formed out of the writings and/or words of the parties, as opposed to an implied contract, which is formed on the basis of the actions or conduct of the parties.

Express Warranty   A guarantee made by the seller of goods or services regarding their quality or performance. This warranty can also be based on the words of the seller; it does not have to be in writing to be legally binding.

Extension Agreement   This type of agreement requires a debtor to pay the full amount of the debt, but with extended payment terms.

Extension Clause   A clause providing that under certain circumstances the due date may be extended.

Factoring   The process of selling one's accounts receivable to another company or person (called a *factor*) who then collects the receivables. Factors earn their profits by paying less than the full value of the receivables and then collecting the full value.

Financing Statement   A document filed with an authorized public official that records an outstanding security interest in a particular property.

Firm Offer   An irrevocable written and signed offer regarding the sale of goods, giving assurance to the buyer that the offer will remain open, usually for a stipulated or reasonable period of time.

Fixed Costs   Those costs that do not vary even though the volume of business activity changes.

Fixture   Personal property that is attached to real property in such a way that the law considers the item a part of the real property.

Foreclosure   Action taken to enforce the payment of a debt by a mortgagee upon default; usually results in the mortgaged property being sold to satisfy the claim.

Formal Contract   A contract deriving its validity from the fact that it follows a specific format required by law. Examples are negotiable instruments, contracts on which a seal is required, and formal acknowledgments of a debt in court.

Fraud   Any act of deliberate trickery, deceit, or misrepresentation of a material fact that causes anyone relying on it damages or injury.

Fraud Implied in Law   When a debtor transfers property without receiving reasonable consideration, and when the debtor does not have enough assets left to pay creditors, fraud is presumed to have taken place. The debtor must prove that there was no fraud.

Fraud in Fact   When a debtor transfers property with the deliberate intent to defraud creditors.

Fraud in the Execution   Convincing a person to sign an instrument when the party signing is deceived regarding the basic terms or meaning of the instrument.

Fraud in the Inducement   When a person is induced through misrepresentation to sign an instrument. Still considered fraudulent even though the deceived person knows what he or she is signing and also knows the basic terms of the agreement or contract.

Fraudulent Conveyance   The transfer of property in a way that the conveyance is regarded as defrauding creditors. Example: You sign over to your wife the title to your Mercedes one week before filing bankruptcy.

Funded Debt   This is long-term debt.

Garnishee   A person on whom a notice of garnishment has been served.

Garnishment   A legal notice that requires a third person owing money to the debtor or holding property belonging to the debtor to turn over to the court the property or money in satisfaction of the judgment. State and federal laws limit the amounts that can be deducted from a debtor's wages.

General Partner   The general partner (in a limited partnership) manages and controls all business affairs and is also responsible for the general liabilities of the business.

Good Faith   Honesty in the actions of a person while negotiating a contract or other transaction.

Goods   Movable, tangible personal property that is used as a medium of exchange. Money is an exception.

Guaranty   A pledge to be responsible for an obligation of a debtor in the event of default.

Homestead   Your family residence; the part of the equity in your family residence home that is exempt.

Illusory Contract   An agreement that, when closely scrutinized, lacks mutual obligations. An agreement that consideration is lacking on the part of one party. The result is that both parties to the agreement are freed of any obligation to perform.

Implied Authority   When an agent has authority that is implied by the position the agent holds in the carrying out of his or her duties.

Implied Contract   A contract in which the parties' agreement is implied by their conduct as opposed to one formed by their actual words.

Incidental Beneficiary   A person who receives a benefit from a contract or agreement between two other parties, but who is unable to legally enforce the terms of the contract because the particular benefit is not an intended result of the contract.

Income Statement   A financial report showing the results of a company's operations over a period of time in terms of revenues, expenses, and net income.

Independent Contractor   An individual hired by someone else to perform work in a manner and method that are not under the control of the employer.

Indirect Collection   The collection of a debt by a creditor, even though the debt has been assigned to another agent by the creditor.

Informal Contract   A contract that does not depend on a specific format to be valid.

Injunction   A court decree preventing a person from performing a certain act or requiring a person to perform a certain act.

Innocent Misrepresentation   A false statement that causes another damages but is not known to be false by the one making the statement.

Insolvency   Under bankruptcy law, the financial condition of a debtor when assets at fair market value are less than debts and liabilities. However, some statutes define insolvency as the point at which a debtor is unable to pay his or her bills when they normally become due.

Installment Note   A note by which the principal and interest are paid in installments at designated times until paid in full.

Inventory Turnover   A figure representing the number of times in a year the inventory investment is turned over. It is calculated by dividing the cost of goods sold by the average inventory amount.

Involuntary Case   A liquidation proceeding that is initiated by a group of unpaid creditors under bankruptcy law.

Irrevocable Offer   A proposal or offer that cannot be legally withdrawn without liability to the offeror.

Judgment, Execution of   The process by which a creditor obtains a writ directing a sheriff or other officer to seize nonexempt property of the debtor and sell it to satisfy the judgment.

Judgment Note   A legal document that authorizes, upon default, immediate entry of judgment by a court without due process of service or trial. Many states have discontinued or restricted the use of such notes.

Junior Security Interest   A security interest or right that is subordinate to another interest.

Landlord's Lien   The right a landlord has to seize and sell a tenant's personal property for nonpayment of rent. The law differs from state to state.

Leasehold   The interest obtained by a lessee under a lease.

Legal Detriment   A required part of any contractual consideration, it means that the promisee promises or does something that he or she is not legally required to do or does not do something that he or she does have a legal right to do.

Legal Impossibility of Performance   When an event takes place after a contract is made that makes performance under the terms of the contract no longer possible. The event legally discharges the obligations.

Legal Rate of Interest   An interest rate that is set by statute when a specific rate is not stated but there is the intent to pay interest. This legal rate is also implied by law where there is the duty to pay interest in spite of any agreement to the contrary. In this latter circumstance, the rate is often called the *judgment rate*. A judgment rate is a rate of interest set by a court to be paid by a defendant until the judgment is satisfied.

Legal Title   Title representing legal ownership of assets or property.

Lessee   The individual who leases (rents) property from a lessor (landlord).

Lessor   The person who leases property to the lessee. The lessor is frequently called the *landlord*.

Lien   A legal claim on a debtor's property for the purpose of securing payment of a debt.

Lien Creditor   A creditor who can legally attach the property of a debtor, including an assignee for the benefit of creditors, a trustee in bankruptcy, or a receiver in equity.

Limitation of Remedies   A stipulation in a sales contract that limits the remedies available to one of the parties to the contract. A common use is a limitation placed by the seller on what a buyer can do when a warranty is breached.

Limited Partner   A part owner of a business who has no control or authority over the business. A limited partner's liability is limited to the amount invested in the partnership.

Liquidated Damages   A sum of money that is agreed on by both parties to a contract before an actual dispute arises.

Liquidated Debt   A debt that is settled and undisputed; a debt for which there is no basis for dispute regarding its existence or amount.

Liquidation   The conversion of assets to cash and the distribution of the proceeds to creditors and or owners.

Liquidation Preference   The preferred shareholder's priority over holders of common stock when the assets of a corporation are distributed on the dissolution or liquidation of corporate assets.

Liquidation Proceeding   In bankruptcy law, a process in which the debtor's assets are sold to pay off creditors and the debtor is discharged from any further obligation to pay the debts.

Lockbox Plan   To reduce mail and check clearing delays in the process of collecting receivables. As an example, a company has its customers send all payments to a nearby post office box where the checks are picked up by a local bank, cleared, and the proceeds wired to the company's main bank.

Long-Arm Statutes   Laws that enable a plaintiff to initiate legal action and obtain a court judgment in his or her home state against a defendant from another state.

Maker   The individual who draws up and executes a promissory note or a certificate of deposit.

Management by Exception   The practice of concentrating the manager's attention on those operations that deviate from the planned or expected results.

Markup Percentage   The amount of gross profit shown as a percentage of sales.

Maturity   The time when a debt or obligation is due.

Mechanic's Lien   A lien against real property for labor, services, or materials used to improve or repair the property.

Meeting of Creditors   A meeting that takes place about one month after the debtor files bankruptcy. During this meeting, the trustee asks the debtor questions about his or her property. The creditors may also ask questions about their claims or dispute the discharge of certain debts.

Mirror Image Rule   A contract law principle in which the validity of a contract is derived from the acceptance adhering exactly to the offer made. This means that the acceptance of an offer, when made according to the exact term, makes the contract a valid one under the law.

Modification   A mutually agreed-upon change in an existing contract or obligation that does not omit any necessary elements of the original agreement, which would render it invalid.

Mortgage   The agreement that conveys a lien on a property to a creditor.

Mortgagee   The creditor (one who receives the payments) in a mortgage agreement.

Mortgagor   The debtor (who makes the payments) in a mortgage agreement.

Motion to Dismiss   The motion filed by a defendant claiming that the complaint does not state a legally recognizable claim. In other words, there is no legal cause for the action against the defendant.

Mutuality of Obligation   A contract law principle that means that both parties to a contract must obligate themselves in order for either to be legally obligated.

Negligence   The failure to exercise the standard of care that would be considered reasonable under the circumstances, when this failure results in damage or injury to another person.

Nominal Damages   A situation in which a court awards monetary damages for a breach of contract but no financial loss has been proved.

Nondischargeable Debt   A debt that cannot be forgiven in bankruptcy proceedings. The debtor will still be required to pay a nondischargeable debt after filing bankruptcy.

Nonexempt Property   Property that a debtor loses in bankruptcy proceedings.

Note   An instrument in which one party promises to pay to another party a specified sum of money on a set date.

Novation   Occurs when an existing agreement or contract is replaced by a new agreement, assuming that the prior contract is a valid one and also that the new contract is proper and valid.

Obligation   A legal duty to do or not to do a specific action. The most common obligations arise out of agreements or contracts or by operation of law.

Offer   A proposal made by an offeror that shows a clear intent to enter into a legally binding agreement on clear and definite terms.

Option   An offer that cannot be revoked. It is formed by a contract with valid consideration.

Option Contract   A contract in which consideration is given to the offeror by the offeree in exchange for a pledge to keep the offer open, usually for a stipulated period of time.

Output Contract An agreement in which a buyer contracts to buy all or a set amount of a seller's product or services and the seller also agrees to sell these goods or services to the buyer.

Partnership An association of two or more persons who operate a business enterprise as co-owners.

Payment Against Documents A contract stipulation term that requires the receiver of goods to pay for the goods upon receipt of documents of title whether or not the goods have actually been received.

Payment Reduction Record A record of payments made to creditors. It should include dates, check numbers, and a running balance.

Perfection The principle by which a priority claim against the collateral of a debtor is given to a secured party through giving notice of the security interest. Example: A leasing company receives priority over a bank if it is the first to notify a debtor of its intent to repossess certain leased equipment.

Performance The action of performing a promise or obligation as agreed on in a contract. When performance is completed by both parties to a contract, the contract is discharged (finished).

Personal Guarantee A guarantee of payment of a loan in which one's personal assets are pledged as well as one's business assets. This type of loan guarantee effectively penetrates the corporate shield from personal liability by giving a lender access to a corporate officer's personal assets, home, savings, and so on.

Personal Property Any property not classified as real property—often called *moveables*. May be tangible (auto) or intangible (shares of stock).

Piercing the Corporate Veil A legal action that bypasses the separate legal corporate entity and reaches to the individual owners of the corporation and holds them personally liable.

Plaintiff The person who begins a legal action.

Pledge A transfer of personal property from a debtor to a creditor as security for a debt.

Preference The transfer of property or payment of money by a debtor to one or more creditors in a way that favors certain creditors. A trustee in bankruptcy can set aside preferential transfers if the creditors knew that the debtor was insolvent, and if the transfers happened within 90 days (one year for insiders) of the filing of a bankruptcy petition.

Private Offering   An offering to sell stock in a business to a small number of selected investors. A private offering is not subject to as many governmental regulations as a public offering.

Private Trustee   A court-appointed specialist, often a lawyer, an accountant, or a personal finance specialist, who supervises the bankruptcy procedures.

Promissory Note   A written promise by one person to another to pay a certain sum of money on demand.

Property (for Bankruptcy Purposes)   All property and moneys belonging to a debtor, including the right to receive money or property in the future.

Punitive Damages   A sum of money awarded as a punishment for the violation of certain legal rights. A plaintiff must prove that actual dollar losses are directly caused by the wrong before punitive damages will be awarded by a court.

Purchase Money-Secured Loan   A secured debt owed to the seller or financial institution that loaned money to buy property.

Quasi Contract   A contract imposed on the parties by law in order to prevent unjust enrichment, even though there was no intent to enter into a contract (also called an *implied-in-law contract*).

Quick Ratio   Current assets minus inventory, divided by current liabilities. Also called the "acid test."

Real Property   Land and most things that are erected on it or attached to it, including shrubs and trees.

Reasonable Definiteness   The requirement that a contract contain reasonable clarity so that a court can determine what are the parties' obligations and rights or whether a breach has occurred.

Receiver   A person appointed by a court to manage a business or other assets for creditors or others who may ultimately be entitled to the assets.

Recision   One of the ways of nullifying a contract.

Release   The act of surrendering or relinquishing some claim privilege or right. If there is deception on the part of a debtor in obtaining a release, the release is invalid and is not legally binding. A release implies that there is a mutual agreement between the creditor and the debtor. A release may be either written or oral.

Reorganization Case   A Chapter 11 bankruptcy procedure under which a company is reorganized and its debt is restructured so that the business may continue operations.

SBA Guaranteed Loan   A small business loan usually made by a bank and guaranteed (up to 90 percent) by the Small Business Administration, which is a government agency. This type of loan is commonly for a longer time period (seven to twenty-five years) than a commercial bank loan.

Secured Debt   A debt arising from a written security agreement by which a debtor pledges certain property as security for the repayment of the debt. Often it is necessary to pay off all or a portion of the debt in order to retain the property (even if it is exempt property) after bankruptcy.

Secured Party   The seller, lender, or other person who holds a security interest.

Security Agreement   A contract between a debtor and a secured party.

Security Interest   The right or interest in property held by a secured party to guarantee the payment of a debt.

Seed Capital   Small sums of money usually given to new business firms in order to help them get started.

Sewer Service   The (illegal) practice of dumping a court summons in the trash instead of serving this legal notification to a debtor. The process server then (illegally) warrants that the papers have actually been served according to law. The result is that one finds oneself the recipient of a court judgment without ever knowing a complaint was filed.

Specific Performance   A court decree that requires a person to perform his or her part of a contract when damages are not sufficient as a remedy.

Sublease   A lease granted by a lessee to another person of all or a part of a leased property, as compared to an assignment of a lease, in which the lessee transfers the entire unexpired term of the lease to a third party.

Substantial Performance   The principle that states that an individual who has performed substantially all of a contract in good faith, and with only slight alterations, has adequately performed the contract and can recover the contract price minus any damages resulting from the slight alterations of the contract's terms.

Summary Judgment   A judgment (before a trial) for one party in a lawsuit, when there are no disputed issues that would require a court trial.

Summons   The cover sheet to a lawsuit. It means basically, "Hear ye, hear ye, you are being sued!" An order that is served to a defendant, notifying that person of the cause of an action claimed by the plaintiff and the requirement of the defendant to answer the summons.

Surety   A person or business that agrees to be responsible for a debt of another by becoming legally liable for the debt if there is a default.

Tangible Assets   Physical assets as opposed to intangibles such as goodwill or patents.

Tender   A formal offer to pay money or perform any other action that is required under the terms of a contract.

Termination of Contract   In general, a contract remains in force until terminated. Usually termination occurs when the terms of a contract are completed. When a contract is terminated because one party breaches its terms, the other party may sue for damages and also terminate the contract. This simply means that if you break a contract, you can be sued.

Time Is of the Essence   A phrase often found in contracts that requires performance within a designated period of time.

Tort   Any private or civil wrong by act or by omission committed by one person against another (but not breach of contract).

Tort of Conversion   A person's illegal interference with the right of another individual's use or possession of his or her personal property.

Trade Credit   Credit given to your business by your suppliers.

Trend Analysis   A method of financial statement analysis in which a comparison of the same item is made for two or more years.

Trustee in Bankruptcy   The court-appointed person in charge of a bankruptcy. It is the trustee's job to convert (sell) all the debtor's nonexempt property and divide the proceeds among the creditors.

Unconscionable Contract   A contract that contains a clause or is in its entirety obviously unfair so that a court will refuse to enforce its terms.

Unenforceable Contract   Usually a valid contract, but one that cannot be enforced by a court because of a failure to meet some particular legal requirement.

Unilateral Mistake   A mistake where only one party to a contract is in error under the terms of the contract.

Unliquidated Debt   A debt disputed as to its existence or amount.

Unsecured Debt   Any debt that is not secured.

U.S. Trustee   The branch of the U.S. Department of Justice that administers the bankruptcy system and acts as a watchdog for fraud and abuse.

Variable Costs   Those costs that react in proportion to changes in volume of business activity.

Venture Capital   Investments made by professional investors to fund start-up companies or rapidly expanding companies that have growth potential.

Voidable Contract   A contract from which either party may choose to withdraw without liability.

Voidable Transfer   A transfer by a bankrupt debtor that can be set aside by a trustee.

Voluntary Case   A proceeding under the Bankruptcy Act that is initiated by the debtor, not creditors.

Writ of Execution   A court order to sell a defendant's nonexempt property in order to satisfy a judgment.

Working Capital   The excess of current assets over current liabilities; the money required to keep a business operating.

Notes

Introduction

1. Dun & Bradstreet, 225 Broadway St., New York, NY 10007.
2. Ibid.
3. Federal Reserve Board, Washington, D.C., 1990.
4. Clerk's Office, U.S. Bankruptcy Court, Central District of California.
5. An ancient Sufi folktale.

Chapter 1. Alternatives to Bankruptcy

1. Sidney Rutberg. *Ten Cents on the Dollar—The Bankruptcy Game.* New York: Simon & Schuster, 1989.
2. Williams J. Donovon. "Hard Times: This Recession Already Longer and Getting Deeper Than Any in 20 Years." *The Providence Journal Bulletin,* February 24, 1991, v. 107, n. 8, p. 1.
3. Laura Jereski and Jason Zweig, "Corporate Restructuring." *Forbes,* March 1991.
4. Tom Curry and William McWhirter, "Forgive Us Our Debts." *Newsweek,* May 1990, pp. 61–62.
5. Laura Jereski and Jason Zweig, "Corporate Restructuring." *Forbes,* March 1991.
6. Robert J. Samuelson. "Debt." *Newsweek,* December 31, 1990, pp. 22–23.
7. Larry Reibstein and David Pauly, "The Loud Clank of Junk." *Newsweek,* September 1989, pp. 32–33.
8. Ibid.
9. "Bankruptcy and Other Debt Cancellation, Internal Revenue Service, Publication 908, Corporations: Equity for Debt Rules, 1992, p. 5.
10. U.S. Bankruptcy Court, Clerk's Office, Central District of California.
11. "Valuation—How Much Is Your Business Worth? Your Bottomline." Reprinted with permission of Paychex, Inc., Rochester, New York, April 1988, pp. 2–7.
12. Tom Curry and William McWhirter, "Forgive Us Our Debts." *Newsweek,* May 1990, pp. 61–62.
13. Ibid.

Chapter 2. Self-Reorganization: Getting Started

1. Adapted from Indries Shah, *The Subtleties of the Inimitable Mulla Nasrudin.* New York: E. P. Dutton. 1973, p. 32.

Chapter 3. What To Do If You Are Sued

1. United States Bankruptcy Court, Denver, Colorado, 28 UCC Rep. 534 (1980).

Chapter 4. There Is a Better Way

1. Walter Meigs, R. Whittington, and Robert Meigs, *Principles of Auditing.* Homewood, Ill: Irwin, 1985, pp. 178, 181.
2. Ibid.

Chapter 5. Working with Employees

1. "You Get What You Pay For." *Inc.,* March 1991, p. 92.
2. Joshua Hyatt, "Ideas at Work." *Inc.,* May 1991, pp. 59–64.
3. Ibid.
4. Dean W. Tjosvold and Mary M. Tjosvold, *Leading the Team Organization— How to Create an Enduring Competitive Advantage.* New York: Lexington Books, 1991, pp. 53–54.
5. "Salary Increases." *Hewitt Associates,* Lincolnshire, Ill, 1990.
6. Alan Thurber, "Luby's Cafeteria Opens 8th Valley Outlet Today." *The Arizona Republic* (Phoenix, AZ), May 1990, v. 101, n. 12, sec. D, p. 1.
7. Tim Clark, "People Skills." *Los Angeles Business Journal,* 1990, p. 69.
8. Jill A. Fraser, "Hands on Financial Strategies." *Inc.,* May 1991, pp. 99–102.
9. "You Get What You Pay For." *Inc.,* March 1991, p. 92.
10. Ellyn E. Spragins, ed., "Hands on Managing People." *Inc.,* May 1991, pp. 93–96.
11. "1990 Survey of Selling Costs." *Sales and Marketing Management,* New York, 1990.
12. James Brice, "After Health Insurance, Many Firms Await Profits Before Adding Benefits." *Los Angeles Business Journal,* December 1990, p. 66.
13. Nathaniel Gilbert, "Healthy Choice." *Entrepreneur,* March 1991, pp. 172–175.
14. Ibid.
15. Martha E. Mangelsdorf, "Safety in Numbers." *Inc.,* May 1991, pp. 24–25.
16. Ellyn E. Spragins, ed., "Hands on Managing People." *Inc.,* May 1991, pp. 93–96.

Chapter 6. Working with Creditors and Suppliers

1. Bruce G. Posner, ed., "Hands on Banking and Capital." *Inc.,* May 1991, pp. 89–92.

2. Ibid., pp. 99–102.
3. Bruce G. Posner, ed., "Hands on Banking and Capital." *Inc.,* May 1991, pp. 89–92.
4. Simonson, Donald G., "The Banking Business: 1992," United States Banker, v. 102, n 7, pp. 51–53, July 1992.
5. Paul Feeley, "Informal Investors Provide Expertise in Your Industry as Well as Money." *Los Angeles Business Journal,* 1990, pp. 55.

Chapter 7. Working with Customers

1. Maurice Mandell, *Marketing.* Englewood Cliffs, NJ: Prentice-Hall, 1985.
2. Mark Henricks. "Satisfaction Guaranteed." *Entrepreneur,* May 1991, pp. 120–125.
3. Ibid.
4. Wirt M. Cook, "Growing a Business." *Entrepreneur,* May 1991, pp. 38–39.
5. Ibid.
6. Ibid.
7. Susan Stocker, "Selling Social Issues with the Product." *Washington Business Journal,* April 1989, v. 7, no. 48, sec. 1, p. 1.
8. Wirt M. Cook, "Growing a Business." *Entrepreneur,* May 1991, pp. 38–39.
9. Tom Richman, ed., "Hands on Sales and Marketing." *Inc.,* May 1991, pp. 85–88.

Chapter 9. The Bankruptcy Path

1. The American Bankruptcy Institute.
2. "Volatile Heritage." *Online Services/Information Access Company,* Foster City, CA, 1992.
3. "Hospital or Morgue." *Forbes,* November 12, 1990, p. 186.
4. Ibid.
5. Daniel M. Morris and Edward C. Dobbs, *Small Business Reports, UMI/Data Courier (ABI Inform),* March 1992, pp. 15–19.

Epilogue

1. Susan Stocker, "Selling Social Issues with the Product." *Washington Business Journal,* April 1989, v. 7, no. 48, sec. 1, p. 1.
2. Ibid.

Bibliography

Albrecht, Donna G. "Resources Guide." *Entrepreneur,* May 1991, pp. 182–184.

"Bankruptcy Expense." *Time,* March 1990.

Bartolome, Fernando. "Nobody Trusts the Boss Completely—Now What?" *Harvard Business Review,* Mar./Apr. 1989, p. 135.

Begley, Sharon, and Mary Hager. "Adam Smith Turns Green." *Newsweek,* June 1991, pp. 60–62.

Bladen, Ashby. "Recessions Are Passé." *Forbes,* Apr. 18, 1988, p. 114.

Blanchard, Kenneth, and Spencer Johnson. *The One Minute Manager.* New York: Berkley Books, 1982.

Brabec, Barbara. *Homemade Money.* White Hall, VA: Betterway Publications, 1986.

Brice, James. "After Health Insurance, Many Firms Await Profits Before Adding Benefits." *Los Angeles Business Journal,* 1990, p. 66.

Brigham, Eugene F. *Fundamentals of Financial Management.* New York: The Dryden Press, 1983.

Bruck, Connie. *The Predator's Ball.* New York: Penguin Books, 1989.

Brummet, Lee R., and Jack C. Robertson. *Cost Accounting for Small Manufacturers.* Washington, DC: U.S. Small Business Administration, 1979.

Clark, Tim. "People Skills. *Los Angeles Business Journal,* 1990, p. 69.

Congdon, Tim. *The Debt Threat.* New York: Basil Blackwell, 1988.

Cook, Wirt M. "Growing a Business." *Entrepreneur,* May 1991, pp. 38–39.

Drucker, Peter. "Permanent Cost Cutting." *The Wall Street Journal,* Jan. 11, 1991, col 4, p. A10(W), P.A10(E).

Epstein, David G. *Debtor-Creditor Law in a Nutshell.* St. Paul: West Publishing, 1986.

Ewing, David W. "Will Business Default?" *Harvard Business Review,* Nov./Dec. 1982, p. 114.

Feeley, Paul. "Informal Investors Provide Expertise in Your Industry as Well as Money." *Los Angeles Business Journal,* 1990, p. 55.

Fischer, Paul M., and William J. Taylor. *Advanced Accounting.* West Chicago, South-Western Publishing Co., 1986.

Fraser, Jill. "Hidden Cash." *Inc.,* Feb. 1991, pp. 81–82.

Friedman, Milton, and Anna J. Schwartz. *A Monetary History of the United States, 1867–1960.* Princeton, NJ: Princeton University Press, 1971.

Galanoy, Terry. *Charge It—Inside the Credit Card Conspiracy.* New York: G. P. Putnam's, 1980.

Gatling, Luther R. "On the Rise: A New Breed of Debtors." *New York Times,* Dec. 20, 1978, p. C1.

Gilbert, Nathaniel. "Healthy Choice. *Entrepreneur,* Mar. 1991, pp. 172–175.

Greenwald, John. "The Profits of Doom." *Time,* Mar. 1990, pp. 41–42.

"Hands on Financial Strategies." *Inc.,* May 1991, pp. 99–102.

Heilbroner, Robert L., and Lester C. Thurow. *Understanding Microeconomics.* Englewood Cliffs, NJ: Prentice-Hall, 1984.

Henricks, Mark. "Satisfaction Guaranteed." *Entrepreneur,* May 1991, pp. 120–125.

Hodgson, Roger S. *Direct Mail and Mail Order.* Chicago: Dartnell Corporation, 1974.

"Hospital or Morgue." *Forbes,* Nov. 12, 1990, p. 186.

Howell, Rate A., and John R. Allison. *Business Law Text and Cases.* Chicago: Dryden Press, 1985.

Hyatt, Joshua. "Ideas at Work." *Inc.,* May 1991, pp. 59–64.

"The Ideal Collection Letter." *Inc.,* Feb. 1991, pp. 59–61.

Jereski, Laura, and Jason Zweig. "Step Right Up Folks." *Forbes,* Mar. 4, 1991, pp. 74–78.

Julian, Frank G., and Helmick, Cindy S. "State and Local Tax Issues in Bankruptcy Reorganizations." *Corporate Taxation,* v5n1, pp. 5–11, May/June 1992.

Killough, Larry N. *Cost Accounting, Concepts and Techniques for Management.* New York, West Publishing Company, 1984.

Kosel, Janice. Bankruptcy, Do It Yourself. Berkeley, CA: Nolo Press, 1986.

Kulin, Joseph. "Your Money or Your Life." *Parabola,* Spring 1991, p. 53.

Lernoux, Penny. *In Banks We Trust.* New York: Penguin Books, 1986.

Lever, Harold, and Christopher Huhne. *Debt and Danger: The World Financial Crisis.* New York: Atlantic Monthly Press, 1986.

Lewis, Herschell G. *Direct Mail Copy That Sells.* Englewood Cliffs, NJ: Prentice-Hall, 1984, p. iii.

Linden, Dana W., and Vicki Contaveski. " Incentivize Me, Please." *Forbes,* May 1991, pp. 208–212.

Malabre, Alfred L., Jr. *Beyond Our Means.* New York: Random House, 1987.

Mandell, Maurice I. *Marketing.* Englewood Cliffs, NJ: Prentice-Hall, 1985.

Mangelsdorf, Martha E. "Safety in Numbers." *Inc.,* May 1991, pp. 24–25.

Maturi, Richard J. "Preventative Medicine." *Entrepreneur,* May 1991, pp. 135–140.

McCarroll, Thomas. "Whose Bright Idea?" *Time,* June 10, 1991, pp. 42–43.

McClain, Jeannette. "How Safe Is Your Bank?" *Silvia Porter's Personal Finance,* 1990, p. 175.

Meigs, Walter, and Robert Meigs. *Principles of Auditing.* Homewood, IL: Irwin, 1985.

Morris, Daniel M., and Edward C. Dobbs. "A Package Deal." *Small Business Reports, UMI/Data Courier,* March 1992, pp. 15–19.

"Motivating on the Cheap." *Inc.,* Apr. 1991, p. 14.

Mundis, Jerrold. *How to Get Out of Debt, Stay Out of Debt and Live Prosperously.* New York: Bantam Books, 1988.

Myers, Neil, and Paul Getchell, eds., *Alternatives to Bankruptcy.* New York: Matthew Bender & Company, 1988.

Obey, David, and Paul Sarbanes, eds. *The Changing American Economy.* New York: Basil Blackwell, 1986.

"On Target." *Inc.,* Apr. 1991, pp. 113–114.

"People Skills." *Los Angeles Business Journal,* 1990, p. 68.

"Picture This." *Inc.,* February 1991, p. 77.

Posner, Bruce G., ed. "Hands on Banking and Capital." *Inc.,* May 1991, pp. 89–92.

Printz, Herbert G. "Look to Commercial Banks for Small Business Loans." *Los Angeles Business Journal,* 1990, p. 59.

"Quick Cash." *Inc.,* Mar. 1991, pp. 95–96.

Reibstein, Larry, and David Pauly. "The Loud Clank of Junk." *Newsweek,* Sept. 1989, pp. 32–33.

"A Relationship with Your Banker Can Mean More to You Than Money." *Los Angeles Business Journal,* Dec. 1990, p. 56.

Rich, Thomas, and Marc Rich. "Bad News from America's Banks." *Newsweek,* Dec. 31, 1990, pp. 42–45.

Richman, Tom, ed. "Hands on Sales and Marketing." *Inc.,* May 1991, pp. 85–88.

Richmond, Suzan, and Sarah Young. "Health and Fitness." *Changing Times,* Dec. 1990, pp. 92–93.

Roget's International Thesaurus of Quotations. Compiled by R. T. Tripp. Thomas Y. Crowell, 1970.

Roha, Ronaleen R. "Your Home Business—A Winning Game Plan." *Changing Times,* Feb. 1991, pp. 63–65.

Rosen, Al. *Business Rescue.* Anaheim, CA: Business University Press, 1989.

Rukeyser, Louis, ed. *Louis Rukeyser's Business Almanac.* New York: Simon & Schuster, 1988.

Rutberg, Sidney. *Ten Cents on the Dollar—The Bankruptcy Game.* New York: Simon & Schuster, 1989.

"Salary Increases Surveys." *Hewitt Associates,* 1989–1990.

Samuelson, Robert J. "Debt." *Newsweek,* Dec. 31, 1990, pp. 22–23.

Schumacher, E. F. *Small Is Beautiful.* New York: Harper & Row, 1989.

Schwab, Victor O. *How to Write a Good Advertisement.* New York: Harper & Row, 1962.

Sethi, S. Prakash. *Up Against the Corporate Wall.* Englewood Cliffs, NJ: Prentice-Hall, 1982.

Shah, Indries. *The Subtleties of the Inimitable Mulla Nasrudin.* New York: E. P. Dutton, 1973.

Shames, Lawrence. *The Hunger for More.* New York: Times Books, 1989.

Solomon, Robert C., and Kristine R. Hansen. *Above the Bottom Line.* New York: Harcourt Brace Jovanovich, 1983.

Spragins, Ellyn E., ed. "Hands on Managing People." *Inc.,* May 1991, pp. 93–96.

Stone, Bob. *Successful Direct Marketing Methods.* Chicago: Crain Books, 1975.

"Strategies That Pay Off." *Inc.,* Mar. 1991, pp. 74–78.

Sutton, David, and Jennifer Lindsay. "When All Else Fails, Turnaround Specialists May Be a Firm's Savior." *The Denver Post,* May 23, 1987, p. 6D.

"The Tax-Advantaged CEO." *Inc.,* May 1991, pp. 68–78.

Thompson, Jennifer. "Avoid Woes in Hiring, Firing." *Los Angeles Business Journal,* Dec. 1990,

Tjosvold, Dean W., and Mary M. Tjosvold. *Leading the Team Organization: How to Create an Enduring Competitive Edge.* New York: Lexington Books, 1991.

"Valuation—How Much Is Your Business Worth?" *Your Bottomline* (*Newsletter*), Paychex, Inc., April 1988, pp. 2–7.

Van Cott, Wendy. "Money Management—5 Mistakes You Don't Have to Make." *Changing Times,* Aug. 1987, pp. 27–31.

Walgenbach, Paul H., and Norman E. Dittrich. *Principles of Accounting.* New York: Harcourt Brace Jovanovich, 1980.

"Washington Whispers." *U.S. News & World Report,* 1991, p. 28.

Wasserman, Dick. *That's Our New Ad Campaign.* New York: Lexington Books, 1988.

Weinberger, Casper. "Scrap and Build." *Forbes,* June 24, 1990, p. 242.

Welles, Edward O. "Bad News." *Inc.,* Apr. 1991, pp. 45–49.

"What Price Profit?" *Entrepreneur,* Dec. 1990, pp. 40–43.

"When You're Too Far in Debt." *Money,* Apr. 1987, p. 49.

"Whittling Away the Public Education Monopoly." *Forbes,* June 10, 1991, p. 24.

"You Get What You Pay For." *Inc.,* Mar. 1991, p. 92.

"Your Family Finances." *Changing Times,* Jan. 1991, p. 74.

Acknowledgments

To Shep Brown and Chris Bradford for their input, encouragement, and friendship.

To Jim Heacock, for his enthusiasm, support, and feedback during the formative stages of this book.

To Beth Anderson, for her excellent editing help and assistance in getting the material for this book organized.

To my wife, Terri, who put up with many late nights of writing.

Index